Pat —

I enjoy rea[illegible] like this because [illegible]ge me to lead well.

Every day is an opportunity to change our world by how we'll live. Impact your world as you read the concepts —

Enjoy

Your Brother

Bill

Joshua 3:5

MEN IN LEADERSHIP

ONE MINUTE BIBLE

ONE MINUTE BIBLE

Daily Devotions to Guide Today's Leading Men

BOB BRINER
with LAWRENCE KIMBROUGH

Nashville, Tennessee

One Minute Bible–*Men in Leadership*

Nashville, Tennessee, 37234

0-8054-9153-8
Dewey Decimal Classification: 242.64
Subject Heading: CHRISTIAN MEN

Production Staff
Executive Editor: David Shepherd
Editor: Lawrence Kimbrough
Project Editor: Lloyd Mullens
Design Team: Wendell Overstreet, Anderson Thomas Graphics
Typesetting: TF Designs
Production: Kevin Kunce

Library of Congress Cataloging-in-Publication Data

Briner. Bob.
One minute Bible : men in leadership / Bob Briner ; with Lawrence Kimbrough.
p. cm.
Includes bibliographical references.
ISBN 0–8054–9153–8
1. Christian men Prayer-books and devotions–English. 2. Devotional calendars. I. Kimbrough, Lawrence, 1963– . II. Title.
BV4843.B75 1999
242'.642–dc21
99–15732
CIP

Printed in United States of America
2 3 4 5 6 04 03 02 01
[Q]

CONTENTS

DAY ONE *It All Starts Here*

DAY TWO *Seeking God's Face*

DAY THREE *Time for Action*

DAY FOUR *Share the Vision*

DAY FIVE *A Matter of Time*

DAY SIX *Your Word on It*

DAY SEVEN *Keep on Keeping On*

DAY EIGHT *Downright Upright*

DAY NINE *You'll Do Just Fine*

DAY TEN *The Big Ones*

DAY ELEVEN *Most Excellent*

DAY TWELVE *Up With People*

DAY THIRTEEN *Active Voice*

DAY FOURTEEN *Without a Prayer?*

DAY FIFTEEN *Under Control*

DAY SIXTEEN *Down in Front*

DAY SEVENTEEN *Closer to Home*

DAY EIGHTEEN *A Fair Assessment*

DAY NINETEEN *What? Me, Worry?*

DAY TWENTY *The Balancing Act*

DAY TWENTY-ONE *Good Job, Everyone*

DAY TWENTY-TWO *The Truth Helps*

DAY TWENTY-THREE *Confrontations*

DAY TWENTY-FOUR *Thoughtful of You*

DAY TWENTY-FIVE *The Bible Tells Me So*

DAY TWENTY-SIX *A Word Fitly Spoken*

DAY TWENTY-SEVEN *A Parent's Priority*

DAY TWENTY-EIGHT *Who Knows?*

DAY TWENTY-NINE — *Peace of His Mind*

DAY THIRTY — *Church Service*

DAY THIRTY-ONE — *Work Your Plan*

DAY THIRTY-TWO — *Single Minded*

DAY THIRTY-THREE — *OK, What's Next?*

DAY THIRTY-FOUR — *Talking Points*

DAY THIRTY-FIVE — *Do Unto Others*

DAY THIRTY-SIX — *A Sacred Trust*

DAY THIRTY-SEVEN — *The One You Love*

DAY THIRTY-EIGHT — *Who? Me?*

DAY THIRTY-NINE — *Glory to God*

DAY FORTY — *Rest for the Weary*

DAY FORTY-ONE — *Your Responsibility*

DAY FORTY-TWO — *I'm Not Surprised*

DAY FORTY-THREE — *A Word of Thanks*

DAY FORTY-FOUR — *Routine Service*

DAY FORTY-FIVE — *God's Word on It*

DAY FORTY-SIX — *Say What?*

DAY FORTY-SEVEN — *It's Family Time*

DAY FORTY-EIGHT — *On Loan from God*

DAY FORTY-NINE — *Off Center*

DAY FIFTY — *Watching Your Back*

DAY FIFTY-ONE — *Total Stewardship*

DAY FIFTY-TWO — *Opportunity Calls*

DAY FIFTY-THREE — *Out in the Open*

DAY FIFTY-FOUR — *Sharing the Load*

DAY FIFTY-FIVE — *Honestly*

DAY FIFTY-SIX — *One Day, One Step*

DAY FIFTY-SEVEN — *Open to Anything*

DAY FIFTY-EIGHT	*Careful Cutbacks*
DAY FIFTY-NINE	*Money Matters*
DAY SIXTY	*Ready for Anything*
DAY SIXTY-ONE	*Experience Tells Me*
DAY SIXTY-TWO	*Goaltending*
DAY SIXTY-THREE	*Pure Motivation*
DAY SIXTY-FOUR	*What Do You Think?*
DAY SIXTY-FIVE	*A Matter of Principle*
DAY SIXTY-SIX	*Generous Helpings*
DAY SIXTY-SEVEN	*No Compromise*
DAY SIXTY-EIGHT	*Fear of Trying*
DAY SIXTY-NINE	*Critical Situations*
DAY SEVENTY	*Yes, You Will*
DAY SEVENTY-ONE	*The Little Things*
DAY SEVENTY-TWO	*Outside the Box*
DAY SEVENTY-THREE	*High Minded*
DAY SEVENTY-FOUR	*Encouraging Words*
DAY SEVENTY-FIVE	*Agree to Disagree*
DAY SEVENTY-SIX	*Clearing the Error*
DAY SEVENTY-SEVEN	*Leadership Costs*
DAY SEVENTY-EIGHT	*No Need to Thank Me*
DAY SEVENTY-NINE	*Work in Progress*
DAY EIGHTY	*Check Your Calendar*
DAY EIGHTY-ONE	*The Real World*
DAY EIGHTY-TWO	*Seeing the Change*
DAY EIGHTY-THREE	*Lifelong Learning*
DAY EIGHTY-FOUR	*People Matter Most*
DAY EIGHTY-FIVE	*Passing the Torch*
DAY EIGHTY-SIX	*I'm Counting on Me*

DAY EIGHTY-SEVEN *What About Now?*

DAY EIGHTY-EIGHT *Health Wise*

DAY EIGHTY-NINE *Steady, Boys*

DAY NINETY *In His Presence*

IT ALL STARTS HERE

The call to Christian leadership is a serious one. Leadership makes things happen. Leadership makes all the difference.

THE WORD FOR THE DAY

CHRISTIAN LEADERS FULLY UNDERSTAND THAT THEIR POSITION IS A GIFT FROM GOD, THAT THEIR INFLUENCE IS DEPENDENT ON HIS HELP.

DON'T BE SURPRISED WHEN OTHERS WHINE, COMPLAIN, AND SECOND GUESS. LEADERS ARE PROVEN BY THEIR RESPONSES TO CHEAP SHOTS AND CHALLENGES.

GOOD BOOKS AND TAPES ABOUND ON THE QUALITIES OF LEADERSHIP. BUT THE BEST ONE IS THE BOOK THAT HAS GOD'S WORD ON IT.

MAKE SURE YOU'RE WILLING TO DO WHAT YOU ASK OF OTHERS.

EXODUS 14:10-14, 21-22

As Pharaoh approached, the Israelites looked up, and there were the Egyptians, marching after them. They were terrified and cried out to the LORD.

They said to Moses, "Was it because there were no graves in Egypt that you brought us to the desert to die? What have you done to us by bringing us out of Egypt? Didn't we say to you in Egypt, 'Leave us alone; let us serve the Egyptians'? It would have been better for us to serve the Egyptians than to die in the desert!"

Moses answered the people, "Do not be afraid. Stand firm and you will see the deliverance the LORD will bring you today. The Egyptians you see today you will never see again. The LORD will fight for you; you need only to be still. . . ."

Then Moses stretched out his hand over the sea, and all that night the LORD drove the sea back with a strong east wind and turned it into dry land. The waters were divided, and the Israelites went through the sea on dry ground, with a wall of water on their right and on their left.

LEADERSHIP PRINCIPLE NUMBER 1

EVERYTHING RISES AND FALLS ON LEADERSHIP.

A leader must be calm in the storm. Turbulent times are sure to come, and when they do, it is imperative for a leader to be a calming, steadying influence. Many appear impressive when everyone is cheering, but a storm is always the true test of leadership mettle. Be ready for the storm. Be ready to calm those around you in its midst.

Visible, palpable panic is the telltale sign that the wrong person was given a leadership role. We need to control our own fears and repress any impulse to panic. We need to speak words of reassurance in a calming tone, addressing the problem in a deliberate, measured, effective way. We need to lead through circumstances, not be overcome by them.

Nothing will raise a leader in the eyes of his followers more than when he effectively handles a crisis. Calm leadership in the midst of a storm will do more to establish a leader than most any situation. In the same way the awestruck disciples wondered about Jesus' identity after He miraculously calmed the winds and the waves, your followers will speak of you with greater respect after you have led them through a storm.

Is This Speaking to You?

Let the daunting size of your task and the sheer weight of your responsibility keep you daily at the feet of God.

SEEKING GOD'S FACE

God's will is much bigger than churches and Christian companies. Wherever you lead, you need Him leading you.

THE WORD FOR THE DAY

BAD REPORTS AND DIRE PROJECTIONS CAN BECOME REGULAR FARE IN THE LIFE OF A LEADER. BUT THEY DON'T HAVE TO BE THE LAST WORD.

WHEN YOUR PROBLEMS ARE BIGGER THAN ANY ANSWERS YOU CAN COME UP WITH, DO LIKE HEZEKIAH. "SPREAD IT OUT BEFORE THE LORD."

PRAYER IS MORE THAN A MORNING PASTIME. IT IS AN ALL-DAY RESOURCE FOR HANDLING THE PRESSURES OF LEADERSHIP.

MAKE SURE THAT GOD GETS THE CREDIT FOR TURNING DOOM AND GLOOM INTO GUTS AND GLORY.

2 KINGS 19:9-10, 14-16, 19

Now Sennacherib received a report that Tirhakah, the Cushite king of Egypt, was marching out to fight against him. So he again sent messengers to Hezekiah with this word: "Say to Hezekiah king of Judah: Do not let the god you depend on deceive you when he says, 'Jerusalem will not be handed over to the king of Assyria. . . .'"

Hezekiah received the letter from the messengers and read it. Then he went up to the temple of the LORD and spread it out before the LORD.

And Hezekiah prayed to the LORD: "O LORD, God of Israel, enthroned between the cherubim, you alone are God over all the kingdoms of the earth. You have made heaven and earth.

Give ear, O LORD, and hear; open your eyes, O LORD, and see; listen to the words Sennacherib has sent to insult the living God. . . .

Now, O LORD our God, deliver us from his hand, so that all kingdoms on earth may know that you alone, O LORD, are God."

LEADERSHIP PRINCIPLE NUMBER 2

EFFECTIVE LEADERS ARE SERIOUS ABOUT SEEKING THE WILL OF GOD.

The challenges of leadership are so many, so diverse, and so complex, that no one person can possibly find enough wisdom in themselves to answer all the questions they face. The very nature of leading others in a worthwhile enterprise implies that the tasks of doing so will be bigger than any one man.

Hezekiah was faced with this kind of overwhelming situation. The enemy king was coming, promising to annihilate Hezekiah and his people. This was no idle threat. The wicked king Sennacharib had made a career of making good on his boasts.

But Hezekiah's response offers us one of the most descriptive word pictures of prayer in all the Bible. He took the warring king's letter into the temple and "spread it out before the Lord." He knew that this problem was totally out of his control.

Leaders can mistakenly pride themselves on being able to handle everything, never being rattled by their problems. But wise Christian leaders must always remember that they have a place to turn for the best answers. God sees everything. And we can only see clearly when He shows us what to do.

Is This Speaking to You?

The breakthrough moment in finding the will of God is realizing that you need Him even more than His answer.

TIME FOR ACTION

You've made your plans, thought everything through. Now it's time to put it into practice. Are you ready?

THE WORD FOR THE DAY

THIS IS A RATHER GRUESOME EXAMPLE—(SORRY)—BUT WHEN FACED WITH THE CHALLENGES OF THE DAY, LEADERS MUST RESPOND.

YOU CAN SPOT THE EMERGING LEADERS IN YOUR GROUP OR ORGANIZATION BY SEEING WHO TAKES CHARGE WHEN OTHERS TAKE COVER.

DECISIVE ACTION ALWAYS REQUIRES AN ELEMENT OF BRAVERY.

AS IN JAEL'S CASE, YOU DON'T HAVE TO BE ON THE FRONTLINES TO MAKE SIZABLE CONTRIBUTIONS TOWARD YOUR TEAM'S SUCCESS.

JUDGES 4:15A, 17-21, 23

At Barak's advance, the LORD routed Sisera and all his chariots and army by the sword. . . .

Sisera, however, fled on foot to the tent of Jael, the wife of Heber the Kenite, because there were friendly relations between Jabin king of Hazor and the clan of Heber the Kenite.

Jael went out to meet Sisera and said to him, "Come, my lord, come right in. Don't be afraid." So he entered her tent, and she put a covering over him.

"I'm thirsty," he said. "Please give me some water." She opened a skin of milk, gave him a drink, and covered him up.

"Stand in the doorway of the tent," he told her. "If someone comes by and asks you, 'Is anyone here?' say 'No.'"

But Jael, Heber's wife, picked up a tent peg and a hammer and went quietly to him while he lay fast asleep, exhausted. She drove the peg through his temple into the ground, and he died. . . .

On that day God subdued Jabin, the Canaanite king, before the Israelites.

LEADERSHIP PRINCIPLE NUMBER 3

DECISIVE ACTION IS NECESSARY IN CRITICAL SITUATIONS.

In almost every enterprise or endeavor, there are critical moments. When these moments occur, bold leaders take bold action–bold, not rash–and the wisest of leaders are careful to submit their plans to God. It is important to remember that more opportunities are lost through inaction than by taking the wrong action.

Whether you are running a business or leading a church, defining moments will almost surely come. They will also come in relationships. One of these moments will come as you seek to lead someone to the Lord Jesus. There will come a time to ask for a decision. You may be there for just such a time.

Jesus never advocated playing it safe. By his own life, by his teaching, by what he prepared his disciples to do, he advocated taking risks for the things that matter most.

Leaders must balance the risk against the consequences. As Jim Elliot said, "He is no fool who gives what he cannot keep to gain what he cannot lose." As a leader, you need to understand the times, the specific circumstances, and the risks. Then at important times, in accordance with God's will, you must take those risks.

Is This Speaking to You?

Make your next important decision be the one to seek God's wisdom on your next important decision.

SHARE THE VISION

It may come as second nature to you, but people can't see the big picture the way you do. Paint it with a passion.

THE WORD FOR THE DAY

GIDEON HAD HIS DOUBTS. BUT WHEN THE TIME CAME FOR LEADING THE CHARGE, HE THREW HIS FULL WEIGHT BEHIND THE MISSION.

GOD HAD TRIMMED GIDEON'S ARMY DOWN TO FIGHTING SIZE. SOMETIMES THE VISION CAN ONLY BE REACHED WITH THE RIGHT PEOPLE.

BEFORE YOU CAN REVEAL YOUR VISION, YOU MUST FIRST HAVE IT CLEAR IN YOUR MIND. CAN YOU PUT YOUR PLAN INTO WORDS?

EVEN IN NON-CHRISTIAN ENVIRONMENTS, THIS IS A GOOD TIME TO REVEAL YOUR DEPENDENCE ON GOD.

JUDGES 7:17-22A

"Watch me," he told them. "Follow my lead. When I get to the edge of the camp, do exactly as I do. When I and all who are with me blow our trumpets, then from all around the camp blow yours and shout, 'For the LORD and for Gideon.'"

Gideon and the hundred men with him reached the edge of the camp at the beginning of the middle watch, just after they had changed the guard. They blew their trumpets and broke the jars that were in their hands.

The three companies blew the trumpets and smashed the jars. Grasping the torches in their left hands and holding in their right hands the trumpets they were to blow, they shouted, "A sword for the LORD and for Gideon!"

While each man held his position around the camp, all the Midianites ran, crying out as they fled.

When the three hundred trumpets sounded, the LORD caused the men throughout the camp to turn on each other with their swords.

LEADERSHIP PRINCIPLE NUMBER 4

LEADERS NURTURE A VISION AND AT THE RIGHT TIME DECLARE IT, SO OTHERS CAN RALLY TO THE CAUSE.

A few years ago, popular Christian author Elmer Towns wrote a book called *Say-It-Faith.* In it he makes the proposition that the key to great achievement is *saying* what you believe God wants you to accomplish.

Suppose you ask, "What's the hardest part about saying to a mountain, 'Go, throw yourself into the sea'?" The answer is, the hardest part is *saying* it. It's not hard to cast a mountain into the sea. It's flat out impossible! But miracles happen when someone has the courage to say, "By the grace of God, this shall be done." That's how Joshua brought down the walls. It is how David defeated Goliath. While others cowered in fear, he spoke up and said, "I'm not afraid of that man. My God is greater than he is." He said it first and then *did* it.

Every great enterprise has been started by someone with "say-it-faith." Somewhere along the way, that leader summoned the courage to actually speak the words describing the vision in his heart. Until that moment, it was just a private dream. But when he spoke, faith began to turn into action, and the dream began to approach reality.

Is This Speaking to You?

Give your latest dream some time to grow and develop. And ask God for the right time to bring it into the open.

A MATTER OF TIME

You know how busy you get. But are you using your time effectively? Or does it feel more like time is using you?

THE WORD FOR THE DAY

"COUNTING THE COST" IS A BIBLICAL IDEA THAT APPLIES TO EVERY AREA OF THE LEADER'S LIFE.

JESUS OFTEN USED SIMPLE WORD PICTURES TO CONVEY IMPORTANT CONCEPTS. TRY USING THIS APPROACH IN YOUR OWN COMMUNICATION.

JESUS DEMANDED TOTAL ALLEGIANCE FROM HIS FOLLOWERS. FROM THE LOOK OF YOUR DAILY SCHEDULE, DOES HE HAVE YOURS?

"HE WHO HAS EARS TO HEAR, LET HIM HEAR." DON'T ASSUME THOSE WHO HEAR YOU ALWAYS UNDERSTAND EXACTLY WHAT YOU'RE SAYING.

LUKE 14:28-35

"Suppose one of you wants to build a tower. Will he not first sit down and estimate the cost to see if he has enough money to complete it?

"For if he lays the foundation and is not able to finish it, everyone who sees it will ridicule him, saying, 'This fellow began to build and was not able to finish.'

"Or suppose a king is about to go to war against another king. Will he not first sit down and consider whether he is able with ten thousand men to oppose the one coming against him with twenty thousand?

"If he is not able, he will send a delegation while the other is still a long way off and will ask for terms of peace.

"In the same way, any of you who does not give up everything he has cannot be my disciple.

"Salt is good, but if it loses its saltiness, how can it be made salty again?

"It is fit neither for the soil nor for the manure heap; it is thrown out. He who has ears to hear, let him hear."

LEADERSHIP PRINCIPLE NUMBER 5

LEADERSHIP IS AN EXPENSIVE CALLING. IT WILL COST YOU TIME THAT WOULD BE EASIER TO WASTE.

Since leaders have influence over the lives of others, their responsibility is enormous. Issues that may not matter to others *must* matter to them. "Everything rises or falls on leadership." You could read a thousand books on management and not find a more important principle. In some ways, it is the story of every human endeavor.

Every success and every failure can usually be tracked back to one ultimate source–leadership. It doesn't matter whether you are talking about the corner grocery store of a multinational corporation. Leadership makes the difference. It applies just as much to a seven-year-old boy's soccer team as it does to the New York Yankees. Leadership makes the difference.

The higher you go in leadership, the greater your personal responsibility. All will be judged, but leaders face a stricter judgment. Why? Because they occupy such powerful positions. They will either lead people toward God or lead them astray.

Leaders have great privileges, but greater responsibilities. Many eyes are watching. Don't let them down.

Is This Speaking to You?

As you examine your schedule and make your plans, be sure your activities are lining up with your true priorities.

YOUR WORD ON IT

If you had it to do over again, you would never have promised to do what you said. But you did. So go do it.

THE WORD FOR THE DAY

BE CAREFUL WHAT YOU PROMISE, BECAUSE TRUE LEADERS ARE EXPECTED TO LIVE UP TO THEIR WORDS.

SADLY, PEOPLE ARE NOT ALWAYS WHAT THEY APPEAR TO BE. EXERCISE CAUTION AND DISCERNMENT IN DEALING WITH THOSE YOU DON'T KNOW.

"THE MEN OF ISRAEL DID NOT INQUIRE OF THE LORD." AND THAT'S WHERE THEY MADE THEIR FIRST MISTAKE.

BACKING OUT OF A PROMISE ONLY MAKES THE PROBLEM WORSE—AND MAY CREATE EVEN MORE HARDSHIPS AND HARD FEELINGS DOWN THE ROAD.

JOSHUA 9:3-6, 14-16, 19

When the people of Gibeon heard what Joshua had done to Jericho and Ai, they resorted to a ruse: They went as a delegation whose donkeys were loaded with worn-out sacks and old wineskins, cracked and mended. The men put worn and patched sandals on their feet and wore old clothes. All the bread of their food supply was dry and moldy.

Then they went to Joshua in the camp at Gilgal and said to him and the men of Israel, "We have come from a distant country; make a treaty with us. . ."

The men of Israel sampled their provisions but did not inquire of the LORD.

Then Joshua made a treaty of peace with them to let them live, and the leaders of the assembly ratified it by oath.

Three days after they made the treaty with the Gibeonites, the Israelites heard that they were neighbors, living near them. . . .

But the Israelites did not attack them, because the leaders of the assembly had sworn an oath to them by the LORD.

LEADERSHIP PRINCIPLE NUMBER 6

LEADERS HONOR THEIR PROMISES, EVEN WHEN THEY HAVE BEEN WRONG IN MAKING THEM.

All leaders make bad deals from time to time. The key is to acknowledge your mistakes, learn from them, and then move on.

It is also important to honor your word and your commitments even when you have made a bad deal. Anyone can honor a good deal, one that has great advantage, but it takes a leader of integrity to keep his word when circumstances show a bad deal was made.

Karl Malone, the great NBA power forward, is one of very few players who does not believe in re-negotiating his contract. Many players, although they sign a long-term contract in good faith, want to tear it up when their market value changes for the better. (They never want to re-negotiate downward when that would be appropriate.) But not Malone. If he puts his name on a contract, he is going to honor it. He is a good example.

To be known as a leader who honors commitments has many advantages. The best and most important one is the knowledge that you are being obedient and are living up to the high standard God sets for those who follow him. No business advantage can equal the joy that brings.

Is This Speaking to You?

Have you committed to something, to someone? Promise God you'll learn from it. But first, follow through on it.

KEEP ON KEEPING ON

Some days you don't feel like getting out of bed. Or seeing anybody. That's when you learn where your strength lies.

THE WORD FOR THE DAY

"THE LORD IS NEAR." ALWAYS TRY TO KEEP YOUR DAILY DEMANDS IN ETERNAL PERSPECTIVE.

WHEN UNDER PRESSURE OR OVERWHELMED, MAKE PRAYER YOUR FIRST LINE OF DEFENSE.

THINK OF GOD'S PEACE AS A "GUARD," PROTECTING YOUR MIND FROM SURRENDER AND DISCOURAGEMENT.

HARD TIMES, LEAN TIMES, CHALLENGING TIMES—THAT IS WHERE TRUE LEADERS ARE MADE.

YOU CAN DO ALL THINGS THROUGH CHRIST. ARE YOU LEADING AS THOUGH YOU BELIEVE IT?

PHILIPPIANS 4:4-8, 11B-13

Rejoice in the Lord always. I will say it again: Rejoice! Let your gentleness be evident to all. The Lord is near.

Do not be anxious about anything, but in everything, by prayer and petition, with thanksgiving, present your requests to God.

And the peace of God, which transcends all understanding, will guard your hearts and your minds in Christ Jesus.

Finally, brothers, whatever is true, whatever is noble, whatever is right, whatever is pure, whatever is lovely, whatever is admirable–if anything is excellent or praiseworthy–think about such things. . . .

I have learned to be content whatever the circumstances. I know what it is to be in need, and I know what it is to have plenty. I have learned the secret of being content in any and every situation, whether well fed or hungry, whether living in plenty or in want.

I can do everything through him who gives me strength.

LEADERSHIP PRINCIPLE NUMBER 7

LEADERS REMAIN MOTIVATED IN SPITE OF CIRCUMSTANCES, NOT BECAUSE OF THEM.

Just about anyone can function at a high level when sales are up, their superiors are singing their praises, a new pay raise is in the bank, and everything is going along smoothly.

It takes a true leader, though, to stay focused and upbeat when the outlook is a little less rosy–which, as most of us come to learn over the years, is more often the case than not.

The issue is our expectations, the things we believe to be the natural rights and privileges of leadership. If we expect to be above having to concern ourselves with the detail issues of running a business or overseeing a project, we will become frustrated by the time required for such matters. If we expect people to automatically come to work each day with the same motivation we have, we will be wearied by the effort it takes to involve and include our staffs. If we expect everyone to always think we're wonderful, we'll be blown out of the water when even legitimate criticism comes.

Jesus told us not to be surprised when life was a challenge and people didn't pat us on the back. Leaders must persevere in spite of their circumstances.

Is This Speaking to You?

Next time you're having one of those days, be sure the only reason you're lowering your head is to barge ahead.

DOWNRIGHT UPRIGHT

Not too many people remember the days of black and white. But people who lead with integrity still see things that way.

THE WORD FOR THE DAY

NOTICE THAT GOD WAS THE ONE POINTING JOB OUT TO SATAN. HE IS APPARENTLY WILLING TO LET THE DEVIL TAKE HIS BEST CRACKS AT GOD'S MOST FAITHFUL FOLKS.

DON'T BE SURPRISED WHEN YOUR INTEGRITY IS CHALLENGED. YOU CAN'T KNOW HOW STRONG IT IS UNTIL IT'S TESTED.

THERE WILL ALWAYS BE PEOPLE LIKE JOB'S WIFE HANDING OUT EASY-WAY ADVICE. BE CAREFUL WHOSE COUNSEL YOU TAKE STOCK IN.

"JOB DID NOT SIN IN WHAT HE SAID." WORDS CAN BE A KEY INTEGRITY INDICATOR.

JOB 2:3-5, 7-10

Then the LORD said to Satan, "Have you considered my servant Job? There is no one on earth like him; he is blameless and upright, a man who fears God and shuns evil. And he still maintains his integrity, though you incited me against him to ruin him without any reason."

"Skin for skin!" Satan replied. "A man will give all he has for his own life. But stretch out your hand and strike his flesh and bones, and he will surely curse you to your face. . . ."

So Satan went out from the presence of the LORD and afflicted Job with painful sores from the soles of his feet to the top of his head. Then Job took a piece of broken pottery and scraped himself with it as he sat among the ashes.

His wife said to him, "Are you still holding on to your integrity? Curse God and die!"

He replied, "You are talking like a foolish woman. Shall we accept good from God, and not trouble?" In all this, Job did not sin in what he said.

LEADERSHIP PRINCIPLE NUMBER 8

STRONG LEADERS MUST BE WILLING TO STAND ALONE WITH THEIR CONVICTIONS.

A great and venerable American company went down when it sold colored water for consumption by babies and called it apple juice. Many who participated in the scheme received jail terms. No doubt, at least some of the executives involved must have had some concern about what they were doing, but, no doubt, those concerns were not grounded in firm, long-held convictions about right and wrong. When the critical times came, when faced with a very significant moral question, their belief system failed them.

In an age of moral relativism, it is more important than ever to be grounded in absolutes. The time to build a belief system and to practice the convictions which arise from it is well before the questions arise. That is why it is so important to develop mission statements to provide a moral compass for our lives.

Jesus insisted on absolutes. He said that some things are good and others are bad. He said that some things are right and others are wrong. We need to be sure that long-considered, well-thought absolutes govern our lives and are firmly in place when the inevitable crisis comes.

Is This Speaking to You?

If you want to be known as a man of integrity, what are some things you can do today to earn that reputation?

YOU'LL DO JUST FINE

Even confident men can feel underqualified sometimes. Don't make yourself feel worse by trying to be somebody else.

THE WORD FOR THE DAY

TRYING TO "COMMEND OURSELVES" THROUGH ANYTHING OTHER THAN OUR WORK AND LIFE IS A WASTE OF TIME AND ENERGY.

"HE HAS MADE US COMPETENT." GOD IS THE ONE WHO GETS THE CREDIT. AND WE NEVER NEED TO FORGET IT.

"WHERE THE SPIRIT OF THE LORD IS, THERE IS FREEDOM" . . . TO BE YOURSELF, TO BE WHO GOD MADE YOU TO BE.

NOT HIDING BEHIND PRETENSIONS CAN BREAK THE PLASTIC MASK OF THE WHOLE ROOM AND MAKE EVERYONE MORE AT EASE.

2 CORINTHIANS 3:1-6A, 17-18

Are we beginning to commend ourselves again? Or do we need, like some people, letters of recommendation to you or from you?

You yourselves are our letter, written on our hearts, known and read by everybody. You show that you are a letter from Christ, the result of our ministry, written not with ink but with the Spirit of the living God, not on tablets of stone but on tablets of human hearts.

Such confidence as this is ours through Christ before God. Not that we are competent in ourselves to claim anything for ourselves, but our competence comes from God.

He has made us competent as ministers of a new covenant–not of the letter but of the Spirit. . . .

Now the Lord is the Spirit, and where the Spirit of the Lord is, there is freedom.

And we, who with unveiled faces all reflect the Lord's glory, are being transformed into his likeness with ever-increasing glory, which comes from the Lord, who is the Spirit.

LEADERSHIP PRINCIPLE NUMBER 9

BE COMFORTABLE BEING YOURSELF IN ANY SITUATION.

Leadership asks a lot of a man. It presents you with a task bigger than you are. It expects you to do things you never thought you could do. It puts you in new situations that call on every resource of your knowledge and experience.

But while successful leaders are able to enter into these uncharted arenas with confidence and optimism, they must also consider themselves free to admit when they're not sure what to do next. They must be willing to believe that God has put them in this situation knowing full well what their talent level and experience base is, and simply expects them to do their best.

Leaders are only human. You know that better than anyone. And we do not serve ourselves well by pretending to be something we're not, by putting on a false face for our customers or co-workers, or by masking our insecurities if only to maintain our respectability.

Though God is challenging you to become more as you exercise your leadership, He is not asking you to become someone you're not. Sometimes, you show how smart you are by asking a dumb question.

Is This Speaking to You?

Next time the nervous tension of feeling unqualified gets the best of you, just try to be the best you can be.

THE BIG ONES

Decisions and demands can get very fatiguing, but not to those who filter them through a set system of core values.

THE WORD FOR THE DAY

THE TEN COMMANDMENTS ARE OVER 3,500 YEARS OLD, AND STILL RIGHT ON THE MARK.

YOU WOULD EXPECT THE WISDOM OF THE AGES TO BE LONG, COMPLEX, HARD-TO-GRASP. THESE LAWS ARE SHORT, SUCCINCT, STRONG. YOURS SHOULD BE, TOO.

GOD COMES FIRST. HIS WILL MUST BE YOUR PRIORITY IN ANYTHING YOU UNDERTAKE IN LIFE, BUSINESS, OR MINISTRY, IF YOU WANT IT TO GENUINELY SUCCEED.

THESE PRINCIPLES ARE NOT TRUE BECAUSE THEY WORK. THEY WORK BECAUSE THEY ARE TRUE.

EXODUS 20:3-4, 7-8, 12-17

"You shall have no other gods before me.

"You shall not make for yourself an idol in the form of anything in heaven above or on the earth beneath or in the waters below. . . .

"You shall not misuse the name of the LORD your God, for the LORD will not hold anyone guiltless who misuses his name.

"Remember the Sabbath day by keeping it holy. . . .

"Honor your father and your mother, so that you may live long in the land the LORD your God is giving you.

"You shall not murder.

"You shall not commit adultery.

"You shall not steal.

"You shall not give false testimony against your neighbor.

"You shall not covet your neighbor's house. You shall not covet your neighbor's wife, or his manservant or maidservant, his ox or donkey, or anything that belongs to your neighbor."

LEADERSHIP PRINCIPLE NUMBER 10

LEADERS MUST HAVE CORE VALUES, CLEARLY ARTICULATED, EASILY UNDERSTOOD, ON THE MAJOR ISSUES OF LIFE.

There seems to be almost nothing some people won't do. They have no core values to guide them when the time for key decisions comes, so they do what seems right for their own interests at the time. The Ten Commandments, when they are considered at all, are seen as quaint, almost laughable, something out of and for another era. And yet, it is also easy to see the terrible price that is paid when the commandments are broken. In fact, *broken* is the word which best describes people who do not respect the commandments.

Leaders, of all people, need to have a set of core values anchored in the Ten Commandments. Leaders need to be sure that the core values of their enterprise are a living, working, governing policy, not just a statement once made and then forgotten. All involved need to revisit the core values on a regular basis.

The Ten Commandments have stood the test of time. They are God's standard for our lives and our undertakings. Do not ignore them. Make them the foundation for all you do.

Is This Speaking to You?

Do you have a written mission statement for your life? They are essential in helping you stay true to your values.

MOST EXCELLENT

You're on. No dry runs. No practice drills. Today, you are in the spotlight at center stage. Give it all you've got.

THE WORD FOR THE DAY

THE FIRST STEP TOWARD EXCELLENCE IS TO BE GRATEFUL FOR THE GIFTS AND OPPORTUNITIES GOD HAS GIVEN.

THE SECOND STEP IS HUMILITY. "WHO THEN AM I" SOLOMON SAID, "TO BUILD A TEMPLE FOR HIM?" REMEMBER WHO'S REALLY IN CHARGE OF THIS THING.

EXCELLENCE DOESN'T MEAN BEING BETTER THAN EVERYONE ELSE, JUST BEING YOUR BEST.

THE POWERFUL AND INFLUENTIAL WILL NOTICE YOUR HIGH WORK ETHIC. BE SURE THEY KNOW WHO IT COMES FROM.

(SEE PROVERBS 22:29.)

2 CHRONICLES 2:3A, 5-9

Solomon sent this message to Hiram king of Tyre:...

"The temple I am going to build will be great, because our God is greater than all other gods.

"But who is able to build a temple for him, since the heavens, even the highest heavens, cannot contain him? Who then am I to build a temple for him, except as a place to burn sacrifices before him?

"Send me, therefore, a man skilled to work in gold and silver, bronze and iron, and in purple, crimson and blue yarn, and experienced in the art of engraving, to work in Judah and Jerusalem with my skilled craftsmen, whom my father David provided.

"Send me also cedar, pine and algum logs from Lebanon, for I know that your men are skilled in cutting timber there. My men shall work with yours to provide me with plenty of timber, because the temple I build must be large and magnificent."

LEADERSHIP PRINCIPLE NUMBER 11

COMMIT TO EXCELLENCE.

Calling ourselves Christian should automatically entail a commitment to excellence. Sadly, this is not always the case. Far too often we use being *Christian* as an excuse for being less than excellent. This is tragic and reflects poorly on the One we love and serve.

We are not called to compete with others. We are only called to "give our best to the Master." A place to begin is in three very simple areas of our lives.

1. *Speak when we are spoken to.* This means returning our phone calls and answering our mail as soon as possible with the answer someone needs. Remember, Jesus never put anyone on hold, never said, "I'll get back to you on that." His level of responsiveness should be our goal.

2. *Don't lie.* This means doing what we say we will do. It means showing up on time. It means accomplishing a task when we say we will. If you say you will call someone for lunch, do it. Excellence means being careful with the truth.

3. *Say thanks.* Of all the people on the planet, Christians have the most for which to be thankful. We should be the most proficient and prolific at saying thank you.

Is This Speaking to You?

You may not feel like you have the time to do everything well. But doing everything well is what time is for.

UP WITH PEOPLE

Some people are easy to like. Others . . . well, not so easy. But everyone you meet deserves to know that you care.

THE WORD FOR THE DAY

JESUS TOOK TIME TO GET AWAY, BUT HE RECOGNIZED WHEN PEOPLE NEEDED HIM MORE THAN HE NEEDED REST.

THE DISCIPLES FELT THEY HAD FIRST DIBS ON JESUS. BUT HE WAS WILLING TO OFFEND HIS INNER CIRCLE IN ORDER TO BE KIND AND INCLUSIVE TO THOSE ON THE FRINGES.

IF YOU EVER REACH THE POINT WHERE PEOPLE ARE IN YOUR WAY, YOUR LIFE HAS GOTTEN OUT OF PROPORTION.

IT DOESN'T TAKE A LOT OF TIME TO SHOW PEOPLE YOU CARE ABOUT THEM. THEY'LL SEE IT IN YOUR EYES IF IT'S TRUE.

MARK 6:30-37A

The apostles gathered around Jesus and reported to him all they had done and taught. Then, because so many people were coming and going that they did not even have a chance to eat, he said to them, "Come with me by yourselves to a quiet place and get some rest."

So they went away by themselves in a boat to a solitary place. But many who saw them leaving recognized them and ran on foot from all the towns and got there ahead of them.

When Jesus landed and saw a large crowd, he had compassion on them, because they were like sheep without a shepherd. So he began teaching them many things.

By this time it was late in the day, so his disciples came to him. "This is a remote place," they said, "and it's already very late. Send the people away so that they can go to the surrounding countryside and villages and buy themselves something to eat."

But he answered, "You give them something to eat."

LEADERSHIP PRINCIPLE NUMBER 12

GOOD LEADERS WORK HARD TO DEVELOP THEIR PEOPLE SKILLS.

Call me old-fashioned, but I believe that nearly all our dealings in business are built on relationships. When I go after a prospective client, I do everything I can to establish a relationship. This isn't a ploy to get business. It's a natural extension of who we are–people who delight in building friendships with others. It's what makes business so rewarding. In fact, if you don't really enjoy developing relationships with people, you probably are in the wrong line of work. Business *is* relationships.

I believe that trying not to get personal with people is a cynical and selfish view of business that stems from unscrupulous exploitation of customers, who are seen only as a source of profit. Sure, court your client, make him think you're his friend. But he's important only as long as he buys your product or hires your company for its services. That's wrong.

As Christians, we ought to lead the way in making business more personable. Your work will be more rewarding, and mark my words, someday one of those clients will ask you what it is that makes you seem so personable.

Is This Speaking to You?

You want to reach your goals and objectives. But connecting with other people should be near the top of the list.

ACTIVE VOICE

You have a right to talk as brave and boldly as you want to, as long as you bear the responsibility for acting on it.

THE WORD FOR THE DAY

BEFORE ASKING THE PEOPLE TO GIVE, DAVID DUG DEEPLY INTO HIS OWN POCKETS TO SHOW THE WAY. WHEN YOU ASK BIG THINGS OF OTHERS, BE PREPARED TO DO BIG THINGS YOURSELF.

THE GIFTS CAME WILLINGLY FOLLOWING THE EXAMPLE SET BY DAVID. BOLD ACTION ON YOUR PART WILL BREED SPONTANEITY IN OTHERS.

YOUR DREAMS ARE ONLY AS GREAT AS THE PRICE YOU'RE WILLING TO PAY FOR THEM.

"GREATER LOVE HAS NO ONE THAN THIS, THAT HE LAY DOWN HIS LIFE FOR HIS FRIENDS" (JOHN 15:13).

1 CHRONICLES 29:1-3, 6

Then King David said to the whole assembly: "My son Solomon, the one whom God has chosen, is young and inexperienced. The task is great, because this palatial structure is not for man but for the LORD God.

"With all my resources I have provided for the temple of my God–gold for the gold work, silver for the silver, bronze for the bronze, iron for the iron and wood for the wood, as well as onyx for the settings, turquoise, stones of various colors, and all kinds of fine stone and marble–all of these in large quantities.

"Besides, in my devotion to the temple of my God I now give my personal treasures of gold and silver for the temple of my God, over and above everything I have provided for this holy temple. . . ."

Then the leaders of families, the officers of the tribes of Israel, the commanders of thousands and commanders of hundreds, and the officials in charge of the king's work gave willingly.

Words are important. They are terribly important in every kind of leadership effort. However, without a leadership example to back them up, they soon ring hollow. When a leader does not back up his words with action, both he *and* his words soon become objects of scorn and ridicule. A leader's words, combined with his example of consistent action, produce successful results.

LEADERSHIP PRINCIPLE NUMBER 13

BACK UP YOUR WORDS WITH BOLD ACTION, AND OTHERS WILL FOLLOW.

Both business and church history provide many examples of leaders who did not back up their words with consistent, stirring action. Neither corporations nor churches prosper under this kind of leadership. Leaders must set the pace in tangible, visible ways. Even in the largest corporations, there are very few secrets. If those at the top do not perform up to their rhetoric, it soon shows throughout the organization.

In this passage, David not only articulated the vision, he stepped up with his own resources. Having set a good example, he could then challenge the other leaders to follow. They did. The people rejoiced. David rejoiced. People knew their leader's heart was in his words. That's leadership at its best.

Is This Speaking to You?

Think of some concrete ways you can demonstrate to your team just how seriously you take your shared mission.

WITHOUT A PRAYER?

We tend to think getting an answer from God is the main reason we pray. The main reason we pray is to be praying.

THE WORD FOR THE DAY

EVER FEEL LIKE YOU'RE BOTHERING GOD WITH YOUR REQUESTS? HE SAID HIMSELF THAT WE SHOULD "PRAY AND NOT GIVE UP."

YOUR ADVERSARY MAY BE—A DEADLINE, A BIG DECISION, A THREAT TO YOUR LEADERSHIP, ANYTHING. BUT YOUR APPEAL SHOULD BE FOR GOD'S JUSTICE TO PREVAIL.

THE LORD'S BUSINESS HOURS ARE 24/7, OPEN "DAY AND NIGHT" TO HEAR THE CRIES OF HIS CHILDREN.

COULD IT BE THAT PERSISTENT PRAYER BUILDS MORE FAITH THAN AN IMMEDIATE ANSWER?

LUKE 18:1-8

Then Jesus told his disciples a parable to show them that they should always pray and not give up.

He said: "In a certain town there was a judge who neither feared God nor cared about men.

"And there was a widow in that town who kept coming to him with the plea, 'Grant me justice against my adversary.'

"For some time he refused. But finally he said to himself, 'Even though I don't fear God or care about men, yet because this widow keeps bothering me, I will see that she gets justice, so that she won't eventually wear me out with her coming!'"

And the Lord said, "Listen to what the unjust judge says. And will not God bring about justice for his chosen ones, who cry out to him day and night? Will he keep putting them off?

"I tell you, he will see that they get justice, and quickly. However, when the Son of Man comes, will he find faith on the earth?"

LEADERSHIP PRINCIPLE NUMBER 14

PRAY ABOUT EVERYTHING.

It fell my lot to be one of the first Americans to go into the People's Republic of China after the end of the terrible Cultural Revolution in that country. I was going in, not as an American, but as the head of an international sports organization. A condition of my entering the country was that I go alone. The Chinese were very wary of foreigners in those days.

The evening before I was to board a People's Republic government jet in Tokyo to fly to Beijing, the legendary founder of Sony, Akio Morita, graciously gave me one of Sony's most sophisticated shortwave radios to take in with me. He said, "Once you get in the Chinese jet, you will be completely cut off from any communication. You won't be able to reach anyone outside China. With the radio, you will at least be able to hear from people outside China."

Mr. Morita was wrong. In the isolation of China, I was able to reach my heavenly Father more easily and directly than ever before. I had no phone or fax, but prayer more than sustained me during those strange days. Prayer kept the loneliness at bay.

Is This Speaking to You?

God has more at stake in your prayer than a yes or no answer. Ask Him to do what He needs to do with you.

UNDER CONTROL

Leaders who can make themselves do the right things will come a lot closer to making other people do them, as well.

THE WORD FOR THE DAY

LEADERS SHOULD KNOW THEIR STRENGTHS, BUT ALSO THEIR OWN WEAKNESSES.

IT'S EASY TO BECOME BLINDED TO YOUR OWN SUBTLE SINS, BUT STAYING ACCOUNTABLE TO A GROUP OF GOOD FRIENDS WILL HELP KEEP YOU HONEST.

GOD WILL ALWAYS FORGIVE. BUT LACK OF CHARACTER WILL COST YOU YOUR SEAT OF INFLUENCE.

THE BEST DEFENSE AGAINST SELF-DESTRUCTION IS TO KEEP YOUR HEAD IN THE PROMISES OF GOD. EVERY DAY. EVERY MOMENT.

1 SAMUEL 15:12A, 17A, 19, 24-28

Early in the morning Samuel got up and went to meet Saul, but he was told, "Saul has gone to Carmel. There he has set up a monument in his own honor. . . ."

Samuel said, "Although you were once small in your own eyes, did you not become the head of the tribes of Israel? . . . Why did you not obey the LORD? Why did you pounce on the plunder and do evil in the eyes of the LORD? . . ."

Then Saul said to Samuel, "I have sinned. I violated the LORD's command and your instructions. I was afraid of the people and so I gave in to them. Now I beg you, forgive my sin and come back with me, so that I may worship the LORD."

But Samuel said to him, "I will not go back with you. You have rejected the word of the LORD, and the LORD has rejected you as king over Israel!"

As Samuel turned to leave, Saul caught hold of the hem of his robe, and it tore.

Samuel said to him, "The LORD has torn the kingdom of Israel from you today and has given it to one of your neighbors–to one better than you."

LEADERSHIP PRINCIPLE NUMBER 15

LEADERS MUST ABOVE ALL BE ABLE TO CONTROL THE WAY THEY THEMSELVES LIVE.

Part of the reason we are so vulnerable to sexual temptation is that we are constantly bombarded by two powerful messages. The first says, "If you're not getting yours, you're the only one. Everyone else out there is having fun."

Nonsense! Not everyone is doing it. In spite of the tremendous sexual looseness of our times, many men in business have determined to remain pure, to honor their marriage vows to the fullest, and to obey the Bible. All they're missing is the tremendous guilt, self-loathing, family brokenness, and shame that comes from a promiscuous lifestyle.

The second message is even more potent. It's the "no-harm, no foul" pitch. You're in a city a thousand miles from home. No one will ever know.

Again, this is a lie. The Bible tells us to flee immorality. Flee is an action verb. It means to run, to get out of there. Stay awake. Stay alert. The pure and honest relationship you have with your wife is a precious gift to be protected. Few things on earth rival the feeling of returning home from a business trip and being able to hug your wife with a clear conscience.

Is This Speaking to You?

Your best intentions are no match for the devil's trickery. But he gets weak in the knees when you lean on God.

DOWN IN FRONT

The spotlight isn't always very discriminating about who it shines on. Careful leaders don't take its warmth to heart.

THE WORD FOR THE DAY

PAUL KNEW VERY WELL THAT HIS WORK WOULD BE WEAK AND FUTILE WITHOUT THE HELP OF HIS FRIENDS.

PAUL DIDN'T JUST GIVE THESE MEN PRAISE, BUT ASSIGNED THEM WORK THAT WAS MEANINGFUL. GIVE THE RIGHT PEOPLE A CHALLENGE, AND THEY WILL RISE TO MEET IT.

"PROMOTION COMETH NEITHER FROM THE EAST, NOR FROM THE WEST, NOR FROM THE SOUTH. BUT GOD IS THE JUDGE: HE PUTTETH DOWN ONE, AND SETTETH UP ANOTHER" (PSALM 75:6-7)

RECOGNITION USUALLY FINDS THOSE WHO DO THEIR WORK WELL.

PHILIPPIANS 2:19-25, 29-30

I hope in the Lord Jesus to send Timothy to you soon, that I also may be cheered when I receive news about you.

I have no one else like him, who takes a genuine interest in your welfare. For everyone looks out for his own interests, not those of Jesus Christ.

But you know that Timothy has proved himself, because as a son with his father he has served with me in the work of the gospel.

I hope, therefore, to send him as soon as I see how things go with me.

And I am confident in the Lord that I myself will come soon.

But I think it is necessary to send back to you Epaphroditus, my brother, fellow worker and fellow soldier, who is also your messenger, whom you sent to take care of my needs. . . .

Welcome him in the Lord with great joy, and honor men like him, because he almost died for the work of Christ, risking his life to make up for the help you could not give me.

LEADERSHIP PRINCIPLE NUMBER 16

TRUE LEADERS ARE UNSELFISH WITH THE LIMELIGHT.

Anyone who has faced times of testing and trial (and who hasn't?) will understand what it means to have friends who stand by you during those times. Friends and colleagues who have been there, in the most profound sense, become very precious. Dave Diles, a top sports broadcaster of a few years ago, described the typical fair weather friend as one who is with you "win or tie." There are lots of those kinds of friends. Much rarer and much more valuable are those who are with you "win or lose." Those are to be treasured.

A leader, who has led through tough times and has had followers who have persevered and hung in there with him, needs to be sure to remind them that he has not forgotten them and the things they've done. The equivalent of Jesus' words ("You are those who stood by me in my trials") needs to be reiterated to them from time to time. Too, their steadfastness needs to be remembered by more than words. Just as Jesus conferred on His disciples a kingdom, today's leaders need to be sure to confer tangible rewards as well as praise on those who have served well during tough times.

Is This Speaking to You?

Be thankful for the kind words, but be sure to share the credit. Center stage isn't all it's cracked up to be.

CLOSER TO HOME

Your best chance at training leaders for tomorrow is to start by training the children who live under your own roof.

THE WORD FOR THE DAY

DAVID WASN'T PERFECT, AND HE FAILED HIS CHILDREN FAR TOO OFTEN BY HIS NEGLIGENCE, BUT HIS FINAL WORDS TO HIS SON ARE STRONG ONES: "WALK IN HIS WAYS."

USE ANY CHANCE YOU GET TO LET YOUR KIDS IN ON YOUR WORLD. IT WILL HELP YOU GROW TOGETHER, AND HELP THEM GROW IN THEIR STRENGTHS.

ARE YOUR CHILDREN ALWAYS WATCHING YOU LEAVE, OR GETTING TO WATCH FIRSTHAND HOW YOU LEAD?

YOU ARE RESPONSIBLE FOR HELPING YOUR CHILDREN'S LIVES BE "FIRMLY ESTABLISHED."

1 KINGS 2:1-4, 10-12

When the time drew near for David to die, he gave a charge to Solomon his son.

"I am about to go the way of all the earth," he said. "So be strong, show yourself a man, and observe what the LORD your God requires: Walk in his ways, and keep his decrees and commands, his laws and requirements, as written in the Law of Moses, so that you may prosper in all you do and wherever you go, and that the LORD may keep his promise to me: 'If your descendants watch how they live, and if they walk faithfully before me with all their heart and soul, you will never fail to have a man on the throne of Israel. . . .'"

Then David rested with his fathers and was buried in the City of David. He had reigned for forty years over Israel–seven years in Hebron and thirty-three in Jerusalem.

So Solomon sat on the throne of his father David, and his rule was firmly established.

Whenever possible, take a family member along with you on your business trips–even if you can only afford to do it once a year. That one trip together will remain in your memory forever.

LEADERSHIP PRINCIPLE NUMBER 17

INVOLVE YOUR CHILDREN IN YOUR LEADERSHIP CALLING.

As your salary increases and your children are old enough, take each one separately on as many of your business trips as possible. Not only will you be giving them a tremendous education (travel is a great teacher), but you will solidify your relationship with them. Plus, you won't have to be lonely. Also, I recommend taking your spouse along as often as possible. It's a great way to nurture your relationship, and believe me–it's fun!

Popular radio pastor and author Chuck Swindoll has a ritual he follows when traveling alone. The first thing he does upon entering his hotel room is to set up a picture of his family on the nightstand near his bed. He says each time he sees it, he is reminded of how much he loves his family and of his obligations and promises to them. The photograph probably doesn't make him miss them any less, but helps fill some of the lonely hours with thoughts of his wife and children.

Is This Speaking to You?

You take your leadership skills for granted. But teach them to your children, so they can take them and run with them.

A FAIR ASSESSMENT

Authentic Christian leaders seek neither the spotlight nor the corner, but seek only the place God wants them to be.

THE WORD FOR THE DAY

YOUR ABILITIES ARE A GIFT FROM GOD, GIVEN FOR YOU TO USE, NOT TO APOLOGIZE FOR.

TRUE HUMILITY CALLS YOU TO UNDERSTAND EXACTLY WHERE YOU STAND WITH GOD—TOTALLY DEPENDENT, YET HIGHLY VALUABLE.

IF INSECURITY OR LACK OF CONFIDENCE KEEPS YOU FROM USING YOUR GIFTS, YOU'RE NOT WINNING BROWNIE POINTS FOR MEEKNESS. YOU ARE FAILING IN YOUR DUTY.

"EACH MEMBER BELONGS TO ALL THE OTHERS." EVEN THE LEADERSHIP GIFT IS A GIFT OF SERVICE.

ROMANS 12:2-8

Do not conform any longer to the pattern of this world, but be transformed by the renewing of your mind. Then you will be able to test and approve what God's will is–his good, pleasing and perfect will.

For by the grace given me I say to every one of you: Do not think of yourself more highly than you ought, but rather think of yourself with sober judgment, in accordance with the measure of faith God has given you.

Just as each of us has one body with many members, and these members do not all have the same function, so in Christ we who are many form one body, and each member belongs to all the others.

We have different gifts, according to the grace given us. If a man's gift is prophesying, let him use it in proportion to his faith. If it is serving, let him serve; if it is teaching, let him teach; if it is encouraging, let him encourage; if it is contributing to the needs of others, let him give generously; if it is leadership, let him govern diligently; if it is showing mercy, let him do it cheerfully.

LEADERSHIP PRINCIPLE NUMBER 18

GOOD LEADERS NEITHER THINK TOO HIGHLY NOR TOO LOWLY OF THEMSELVES.

Jesus never varied from His mission. One part of that mission involved making sure people knew who He was and why He came. To that end, Jesus corrected misinformation and always gave God credit and glory.

Leadership by its very nature generates positive comments. The better you do your job, the more praise you receive–and the greater the possibility of being misunderstood and of having flattery go to your head. Some leadership positions need to be sort of glamorized for the enterprise to succeed. Leaders in these kinds of positions need to be especially alert to flattery's seductive nature. To put this admonition in the vernacular, "Don't get sucked in." Or to use the words of Jesus, which are always better, "Woe to you when all men speak well of you" (Luke 6:26).

One of the best weapons leaders can use in order to combat a tendency toward arrogance is to keep in mind a clear picture of Jesus kneeling to wash the feet of His disciples.

Be aware that flattery is a weapon of the enemy. It can lead to arrogance, and arrogance is deadly.

Is This Speaking to You?

Thank God for the myriad of talents He's invested in you. And thank Him more vividly by using them all well.

WHAT? ME, WORRY?

Tomorrow's meeting and next week's deadline are of little importance compared to what God wants you doing today.

THE WORD FOR THE DAY

RUTH DIDN'T GO INTO THE FIELDS SEEKING A HUSBAND, BUT GOD WAS WATCHING OUT FOR HER FUTURE NEEDS WHILE SHE WAS WATCHING AFTER HER DAILY TASKS.

GOD HAS A WAY OF WEAVING ALL YOUR PAST EXPERIENCES, RELATIONSHIPS, AND CONNECTIONS INTO A LIFE PLAN YOU NEVER WOULD HAVE FIGURED OUT ON YOUR OWN.

BE ON THE WATCH FOR "CHANCE" MEETINGS. GOD CAN MAKE GREAT THINGS DEVELOP FROM EVERYDAY MOMENTS.

ORDINARY OBEDIENCE IS THE ONLY REAL PATH TO FINDING GOD'S WILL.

RUTH 2:17, 19-23A

So Ruth gleaned in the field until evening. Then she threshed the barley she had gathered, and it amounted to about an ephah. . . .

Her mother-in-law asked her, "Where did you glean today? Where did you work? Blessed be the man who took notice of you!" Then Ruth told her mother-in-law about the one at whose place she had been working. "The name of the man I worked with today is Boaz," she said.

"The LORD bless him!" Naomi said to her daughter-in-law. "He has not stopped showing his kindness to the living and the dead." She added, "That man is our close relative; he is one of our kinsman-redeemers."

Then Ruth the Moabitess said, "He even said to me, 'Stay with my workers until they finish harvesting all my grain.'"

Naomi said to Ruth her daughter-in-law, "It will be good for you, my daughter, to go with his girls, because in someone else's field you might be harmed."

So Ruth stayed close to the servant girls of Boaz. . . .

LEADERSHIP PRINCIPLE NUMBER 19

DO WHAT YOU OUGHT TO DO EACH DAY, AND TRUST GOD FOR THE RIGHT RESULTS.

When leaders don't know what else to do, they can always do what needs to be done each day, working diligently through their agendas. Most days are going to be like that–get up, do your job, go home, eat dinner, spend time with your family, go to bed. Get up and do it again the next day. This is life most of the time. And yet, it is important to realize that God is weaving an unseen pattern into our lives. As we do the routine well, the pattern becomes more appealing and more useful.

Leaders also find ways to add some extra flair to the routine. A very successful Dallas business executive asks the Lord each day to show him at least two people–one to thank and one to congratulate. To get this done, he sometimes goes to the newspaper to find people who are doing good things for the city or who have accomplished something of worth. Often, they are people right in his office or among his family and friends.

Some say, "Don't sweat the small stuff." God asks us to be careful about the seemingly small matters of life because, in many respects, they *are* life, and we need to make the most of what he has given us.

Is This Speaking to You?

____

____

____

____

____

____

____

____

____

____

____

____

____

____

____

____

____

____

____

____

____

____

If you can already see how you're going to get everything done, you're probably doing something too small.

THE BALANCING ACT

Your life as a leader will always push you beyond your own limits, but be careful that it doesn't push you over the edge.

THE WORD FOR THE DAY

THE CHURCH CAN OFTEN BE THE WORST AT EXPECTING MORE OF US THAN GOD HAS CALLED US TO SHOULDER. **NO** IS AN ACCEPTABLE ANSWER.

A LIFE OUT OF BALANCE WILL EVENTUALLY ERUPT IN AN EXPLOSION OF BLAME, EXCUSES, AND FRUSTRATION.

YOUR ABILITY TO COPE WITH RINGS OF RESPONSIBILITY WILL CAUSE PEOPLE TO ASK WHERE YOUR STRENGTH COMES FROM. INTRODUCE THEM TO YOUR SILENT PARTNER.

"LET ME DO NOTHING TODAY WITHOUT CALMNESS OF SOUL."

—JOHN WESLEY

LUKE 10:38-42
MATTHEW 6:31-33

As Jesus and his disciples were on their way, he came to a village where a woman named Martha opened her home to him. She had a sister called Mary, who sat at the Lord's feet listening to what he said.

But Martha was distracted by all the preparations that had to be made. She came to him and asked, "Lord, don't you care that my sister has left me to do the work by myself? Tell her to help me!"

"Martha, Martha," the Lord answered, "you are worried and upset about many things, but only one thing is needed. Mary has chosen what is better, and it will not be taken away from her. . . .

"So do not worry, saying, 'What shall we eat?' or 'What shall we drink?' or 'What shall we wear?' For the pagans run after all these things, and your heavenly Father knows that you need them.

"But seek first his kingdom and his righteousness, and all these things will be given to you as well."

LEADERSHIP PRINCIPLE NUMBER 20

KEEP YOURSELF IN CONSTANT BALANCE.

In the life of almost every corporate manager and executive, there will be times when you feel like an armed mob is coming after you and your company. Labor unrest, product safety breakdown, critical material shortages, takeover attempts, and the dreaded cash-flow crisis are examples. That's when the effective leader remains calm and provides positive, reassuring leadership.

Next to recognizing the need for calm, the most important thing is to plan for tough times. The wise executive devises carefully drawn crisis plans appropriate to the various challenges that might arise. He will also have a crisis team in place, and each member of the team will know his role. This kind of planning helps ensure calm all around.

Another useful but often neglected calm-producing activity is prayer. This might seem a little mystical to the average business manager. But even spiritual skeptics have noted the empirical evidence of the calm that prayer produces. It is not coincidental that Jesus spent the hours just before his arrest in prayer. Be like Jesus. Stay calm, keep your perspective, be a balanced leader.

Is This Speaking to You?

There's enough time today to do everything God expects. If you simply can't get it done, maybe it's not yours to do.

GOOD JOB, EVERYONE

You may be the one who gets the first round of applause. But be quick to thank the others who deserve the acclaim.

THE WORD FOR THE DAY

PUBLIC STATEMENTS OF THANKS ARE NICE, BUT GOING OUT OF YOUR WAY TO SAY THANKS IN PRIVATE LETS PEOPLE KNOW YOU REALLY MEAN IT.

THANK-YOU NOTES SHOULD BE A STAPLE IN YOUR BRIEFCASE, SO YOU CAN SEIZE ANY SPARE MOMENT TO JOT A QUICK WORD OF GRATITUDE.

THE BEST WAY TO KEEP FROM SOUNDING PHONY IN YOUR PRAISE IS TO NOT BE. CULTIVATE A HEART OF GRATITUDE.

THOSE YOU BLESS AND CONGRATULATE WILL BE MORE RECEPTIVE TO YOUR OCCASIONAL REBUKE.

PHILIPPIANS 4:10, 14-19

I rejoice greatly in the Lord that at last you have renewed your concern for me. Indeed, you have been concerned, but you had no opportunity to show it. . . .

Yet it was good of you to share in my troubles.

Moreover, as you Philippians know, in the early days of your acquaintance with the gospel, when I set out from Macedonia, not one church shared with me in the matter of giving and receiving, except you only; for even when I was in Thessalonica, you sent me aid again and again when I was in need.

Not that I am looking for a gift, but I am looking for what may be credited to your account. I have received full payment and even more; I am amply supplied, now that I have received from Epaphroditus the gifts you sent. They are a fragrant offering, an acceptable sacrifice, pleasing to God.

And my God will meet all your needs according to his glorious riches in Christ Jesus.

LEADERSHIP PRINCIPLE NUMBER 21

WISE LEADERS EMPHASIZE THE CONTRIBUTIONS OF ALL THOSE INVOLVED IN THE ENDEAVOR.

Good leaders understand that they don't need to do it all, really cannot do it all and, even if they could, shouldn't do it all. Quality leaders understand that a fully involved team is always better than one on which there are those who are inactive. The best modern professional sports coaches build their teams in such a way that every player has a role in every game. In the old days, a coach had starters who played every game and substitutes who were basically uninvolved unless called on to replace an injured starter. No more. The best coaches these days have all their players in the action in some way every game. This is the pattern that Paul laid out for the church. It is a pattern that works well in any organized activity. Everyone should have an active role every day. Good leaders make this happen.

Good leaders also honor those whose contributions are vital but often unrecognized. Your leadership is enhanced when you see to it that all your followers are fully engaged at all times. All your efforts will be energized when you give appropriate honor to others.

Is This Speaking to You?

Commit to being a leader who notices people that others take for granted. Let them know you appreciate them.

THE TRUTH HELPS

The only way to know where you need to go–and to know how to get there–is to be honest about where you are now.

THE WORD FOR THE DAY

THE SPIES WEREN'T WRONG IN THEIR OBSERVATIONS, ONLY IN THEIR VISION.

OTHER PEOPLE OFTEN CAN'T SEE THE BIG PICTURE THE WAY YOU DO. AS A LEADER, YOU MUST SEE THE OBSTACLES, BUT WELCOME THE CHALLENGE.

JOSHUA AND CALEB HAD NO GUARANTEES THAT THEIR PLAN WOULD SUCCEED. WITH CONFIDENCE IN GOD, THEY WERE WILLING TO PUT THEIR LIVES ON THE LINE.

YOU'RE ASKING A LOT OF OTHERS. BE SURE YOU'RE WILLING TO GO RIGHT INTO THE FIGHT WITH THEM.

NUMBERS 14:2-4, 6-9

All the Israelites grumbled against Moses and Aaron, and the whole assembly said to them, "If only we had died in Egypt! Or in this desert! Why is the LORD bringing us to this land only to let us fall by the sword? Our wives and children will be taken as plunder. Wouldn't it be better for us to go back to Egypt?"

And they said to each other, "We should choose a leader and go back to Egypt. . . ."

Joshua son of Nun and Caleb son of Jephunneh, who were among those who had explored the land, tore their clothes and said to the entire Israelite assembly, "The land we passed through and explored is exceedingly good.

"If the LORD is pleased with us, he will lead us into that land, a land flowing with milk and honey, and will give it to us. Only do not rebel against the LORD. And do not be afraid of the people of the land, because we will swallow them up. Their protection is gone, but the LORD is with us. Do not be afraid of them."

LEADERSHIP PRINCIPLE NUMBER 22

FACE PROBLEMS REALISTICALLY, WHILE CASTING A VISION OF HOW GREAT THE FUTURE CAN BE.

Unrealistic expectations damage morale, perhaps as much as any negative circumstance you can imagine. This is almost always cited when a follower goes into an unproductive funk or quits. "I thought it was going to be different" or "They didn't tell me it would be this hard" are the kind of statements most often heard when someone bails out of a project. Most people can handle most situations if they have been realistically prepared to face them.

When trying to enlist someone into an effort, it might be tempting to paint an overly rosy picture of the endeavor. Don't do it. Always present the opportunity in the best possible, honest, and realistic light. Overselling might gain more recruits, but it also causes you to lose them pretty fast when the real difficulties of any worthwhile endeavor become apparent.

Certainly it is important to let prospective colleagues see the potential upside, but they should know what will be required of them to reach the sunny shores of success. Those you really want and those who will stay with you through the difficulties will appreciate both the challenge and your honesty.

Is This Speaking to You?

People will follow if you're honest about the problems, fair about the expectations, and confident about the outcome.

CONFRONTATIONS

You are responsible for tending your vision and purpose–and for dealing squarely with those who are endangering it.

THE WORD FOR THE DAY

DEPENDING ON YOUR ARENA OF LEADERSHIP AND YOUR RELATIONSHIP WITH YOUR COWORKERS, YOU MAY NEED TO ADDRESS EVEN PERSONAL ISSUES OF CONCERN.

THE YEAST PRINCIPLE SHOWS HOW EVEN A LITTLE DISCONTENT AMONG THE RANKS TENDS TO POISON OTHERS.

"DO NOT JUDGE, OR YOU TOO WILL BE JUDGED" IS A TEACHING OF JESUS THAT SPEAKS TO PERSONAL INTEGRITY, BUT DOESN'T PRECLUDE US FROM PRACTICING OUR RIGHT—AND OUR NEED—TO JUDGE AND ADMONISH THOSE WITHIN OUR SPHERE OF RESPONSIBILITY.

1 CORINTHIANS 5:1-2, 6, 9-12A

It is actually reported that there is sexual immorality among you, and of a kind that does not occur even among pagans: A man has his father's wife.

And you are proud! Shouldn't you rather have been filled with grief and have put out of your fellowship the man who did this?...

Your boasting is not good. Don't you know that a little yeast works through the whole batch of dough?...

I have written to you in my letter not to associate with sexually immoral people–not at all meaning the people of this world who are immoral, or the greedy and swindlers, or idolaters. In that case you would have to leave this world.

But now I am writing to you that you must not associate with anyone who calls himself a brother but is sexually immoral or greedy, an idolater or a slanderer, a drunkard or a swindler. With such a man do not even eat.

What business is it of mine to judge those outside the church? Are you not to judge those inside?

Wise leaders wait for the right moment, give a sharp rebuke, and then move on. Foolish leaders keep repeating their criticisms endlessly, which leads not to better performance, but to resentment and discouragement.

LEADERSHIP PRINCIPLE NUMBER 23

LEADERS CANNOT BE AFRAID TO CONFRONT THOSE WHO ARE HARMING THE CAUSE.

Good leaders use rebukes, especially the stinging ones, sparingly and strategically. They never use them to tear down or to ridicule for the sake of ridiculing. They always have a positive purpose. That purpose should never be to show how macho or clever the leader is or to give the leader ego gratification. Rebukes should hurt the leader as much as the one being rebuked.

Timing is everything–both in giving compliments and criticisms. Jesus didn't hesitate to challenge His followers when He felt they weren't paying enough attention to what He was saying and doing. But He always did it in a way that preserved their dignity even while driving the painful point home.

Jesus' rebukes were always for both the good of the person and the success of the enterprise. His example shows that a carefully considered rebuke, given with positive results in mind, is a leadership tool not to be neglected.

Is This Speaking to You?

Is there someone whose work and attitude is draining the life out of others on your team? Consider the consequences.

THOUGHTFUL OF YOU

There's work to be done and only so much time to do it, but caring for those around you should be business as usual.

THE WORD FOR THE DAY

THE PRIEST AND THE LEVITE SURELY HAD WELL-WORDED RATIONALES FOR PASSING UP THE MAN IN NEED. YOU MAY HAVE HEARD THEM PASSING THROUGH YOUR OWN MIND A TIME OR TWO.

WHEREVER POSSIBLE, PLAN SOME AIR INTO YOUR DAY. YOU NEVER KNOW WHEN SOMETHING MORE IMPORTANT MIGHT COME UP.

ONE HANDWRITTEN NOTE (JUST A SHORT ONE) CAN DO MORE THAN A DOZEN ENCOURAGING WORDS OR PHONE CALLS.

JESUS SAID, "GO AND DO LIKEWISE." YES, THAT MEANS US.

LUKE 10:30-34, 36-37

In reply Jesus said: "A man was going down from Jerusalem to Jericho, when he fell into the hands of robbers. They stripped him of his clothes, beat him and went away, leaving him half-dead.

"A priest happened to be going down the same road, and when he saw the man, he passed by on the other side.

"So too, a Levite, when he came to the place and saw him, passed by on the other side.

"But a Samaritan, as he traveled, came where the man was; and when he saw him, he took pity on him.

"He went to him and bandaged his wounds, pouring on oil and wine. Then he put the man on his own donkey, brought him to an inn and took care of him. . . .

"Which of these three do you think was a neighbor to the man who fell into the hands of robbers?"

The expert in the law replied, "The one who had mercy on him." Jesus told him, "Go and do likewise."

BRINER NOTES

A leader takes care of his followers and those important to his followers. Those you are leading can only be effective when their needs *and* the needs of their families are met. An effective leader understands this and is sensitive to it. Serve your followers *and* their families.

LEADERSHIP PRINCIPLE NUMBER 24

TAKING THE TIME TO BE THOUGHTFUL OF OTHERS SEPARATES GOOD LEADERS FROM GREAT ONES.

This may sound soft to some hard-driving, goal-oriented modern leaders, but it is truly the ultimate hard-nosed formula for success. By removing obstacles to their focus, you enable your followers to concentrate on their given tasks. As strange as it may seem, the surest way for a leader to succeed is to put others first, including the families of those he leads.

Jesus became personally involved in solving problems–small details for someone with such an important mission. It could be argued that Jesus didn't have the time. But through his actions, he proved that although it is always easier to say, "Take care of this for me," it is often better to say, "Let me take care of it myself." Your followers and their families will remember and appreciate your personal touch.

Is This Speaking to You?

You'll have some unplanned opportunities to be unusually kind today. Why don't you make that part of your plan?

THE BIBLE TELLS ME SO

People can hide big questions beneath the surface of their small talk. Are you prepared to offer the answers of faith?

THE WORD FOR THE DAY

THE WITNESS OF YOUR CHARACTER WILL CREATE OPPORTUNITIES FOR THE WITNESS OF YOUR WORDS. BE READY TO RESPOND.

"ALWAYS BE PREPARED TO GIVE AN ANSWER TO EVERYONE WHO ASKS YOU TO GIVE THE REASON FOR THE HOPE THAT YOU HAVE" (1 PETER 3:15).

GET TO KNOW THE KINDS OF QUESTIONS THAT CUT THROUGH THE CLUTTER, THE ONES THAT OPEN PEOPLE'S HEARTS TO HEAR WHAT YOU HAVE TO SAY.

TRY TO DISCERN WHAT PEOPLE ARE REALLY ASKING, SO YOUR TESTIMONY CAN SPEAK TO THEM RIGHT WHERE THEY ARE.

ACTS 8:26-31, 34-35

Now an angel of the Lord said to Philip, "Go south to the road–the desert road–that goes down from Jerusalem to Gaza."

So he started out, and on his way he met an Ethiopian eunuch, an important official in charge of all the treasury of Candace, queen of the Ethiopians. This man had gone to Jerusalem to worship, and on his way home was sitting in his chariot reading the book of Isaiah the prophet.

The Spirit told Philip, "Go to that chariot and stay near it." Then Philip ran up to the chariot and heard the man reading Isaiah the prophet. "Do you understand what you are reading?" Philip asked.

"How can I," he said, "unless someone explains it to me?" So he invited Philip to come up and sit with him. . . .

The eunuch asked Philip, "Tell me, please, who is the prophet talking about, himself or someone else?" Then Philip began with that very passage of Scripture and told him the good news about Jesus.

LEADERSHIP PRINCIPLE NUMBER 25

CHRISTIAN LEADERS SHOULD NOT ONLY LIVE THEIR FAITH, BUT KNOW HOW TO PUT IT INTO WORDS.

Leaders must be able to face opposition. The ability to hold one's own when faced with criticism builds tremendous confidence in followers. Teachers can teach best in congenial settings conducive to learning, but leaders can teach even in hostile settings when faced with powerful attacks. Leaders are prepared for the inevitable challenges.

Leaders know what they're talking about. They understand their mission and how to articulate it. We live in the media age, in which sound bites often are called for. Leaders must have their sound bites ready to inspire prospective followers.

Certainly Jesus taught in very thoughtful, comprehensive ways, as in the Sermon on the Mount and through His powerful parables. But very often He taught with what we today call sound bites–pithy, potent, precise comments that stopped the debate. Jesus was the ultimate counterpuncher. His opponents struck the first verbal blow, but He always struck the last. By silencing the snipers with His profound responses, He strengthened and solidified His leadership position.

Is This Speaking to You?

As you read the Bible, try to look beyond what it's saying to you and consider how God can help you speak it to others.

A WORD FITLY SPOKEN

Every day you meet people who need your encouragement, your help, your insight, your time. Are you giving it?

THE WORD FOR THE DAY

CHRISTIAN LEADERS SHOULD HAVE ALL THE MOTIVATION THEY NEED TO ACTIVELY SEEK WAYS TO HELP THOSE AROUND THEM: "FOR CHRIST'S LOVE COMPELS US."

"FROM NOW ON WE REGARD NO ONE FROM A WORLDLY POINT OF VIEW." WORK HARD TO SEE PEOPLE'S POTENTIAL RATHER THAN THEIR PAST.

IF YOU WERE A PERSON UNDER YOUR LEADERSHIP, HOW WOULD YOU LIKE TO BE TREATED?

EVEN IF YOUR WORKPLACE DOESN'T BELIEVE IT, REMEMBER THAT PEOPLE'S GREATEST NEED IS THEIR NEED FOR JESUS.

2 CORINTHIANS 5:14-20

For Christ's love compels us, because we are convinced that one died for all, and therefore all died.

And he died for all, that those who live should no longer live for themselves but for him who died for them and was raised again.

So from now on we regard no one from a worldly point of view. Though we once regarded Christ in this way, we do so no longer.

Therefore, if anyone is in Christ, he is a new creation; the old has gone, the new has come!

All this is from God, who reconciled us to himself through Christ and gave us the ministry of reconciliation: that God was reconciling the world to himself in Christ, not counting men's sins against them. And he has committed to us the message of reconciliation.

We are therefore Christ's ambassadors, as though God were making his appeal through us. We implore you on Christ's behalf: Be reconciled to God.

Good leaders care about those who follow them, but *great* leaders get personally involved in helping solve their personal difficulties. In helping a follower, a leader not only shows compassion, but also frees the follower for greater service. The prime example of this is Jesus healing Peter's mother-in-law. He cared not only about Peter, but also about those Peter cared about.

LEADERSHIP PRINCIPLE NUMBER 26

EFFECTIVE LEADERS GET PERSONALLY INVOLVED TO SOLVE DIFFICULT PERSONAL PROBLEMS.

Paul provides some wonderful leadership examples in his appeal to Philemon. Paul was returning Philemon's slave Onesimus to him and offering to pay anything the young man owed him. Too, Paul was very tactful. As an apostle, he could have ordered Philemon to do things his way, but rather he acknowledged Philemon's rights and appealed to him to show Christian kindness and brotherly love.

It is important to understand that true leadership extends beyond formal relationships and official duties. Christian leaders in particular should care for the whole person. This is one of the reasons it is so important to choose your followers very carefully. In a large sense, you are adopting them. They become a part of your family.

Is This Speaking to You?

The easiest course of action is to not get involved. But by making yourself vulnerable, you make yourself valuable.

A PARENT'S PRIORITY

As hard as it is to admit, we can all be replaced. But not as the parents of our children. We're all that they've got.

THE WORD FOR THE DAY

TRAINING YOUR CHILDREN TO OBEY YOU NOW WILL MAKE IT THAT MUCH EASIER FOR THEM TO OBEY GOD LATER.

MAKE TIME TO TALK, AND ALSO TO LISTEN.

HOW WELL DO YOUR KIDS KNOW YOUR LIFE STORY? THEY CAN LEARN A LOT FROM WHAT GOD'S DONE WITH YOU.

GODLY CHILDREN ARE THE BEST INVESTMENT YOU CAN MAKE IN LIFE.

IF YOU CAN'T EXPLAIN YOUR BELIEFS WHERE A CHILD CAN UNDERSTAND, YOU MAY NOT UNDERSTAND THEM ALL THAT WELL YOURSELF.

PSALM 78:1-8

O my people, hear my teaching; listen to the words of my mouth.

I will open my mouth in parables, I will utter hidden things, things from of old–what we have heard and known, what our fathers have told us.

We will not hide them from their children; we will tell the next generation the praiseworthy deeds of the LORD, his power, and the wonders he has done.

He decreed statutes for Jacob and established the law in Israel, which he commanded our forefathers to teach their children, so that the next generation would know them, even the children yet to be born, and they in turn would tell their children.

Then they would put their trust in God and would not forget his deeds but would keep his commands.

They would not be like their forefathers–a stubborn and rebellious generation, whose hearts were not loyal to God, whose spirits were not faithful to him.

BRINER NOTES

LEADERSHIP PRINCIPLE NUMBER 27

NO MATTER HOW IMPORTANT YOUR ROLE, PARENTING YOUR CHILDREN IS MORE IMPORTANT.

Both by His teaching and His example, Jesus underscored the importance of children. It might seem paradoxical, with so much to do in so short a time period, that He would take so much time to talk about children, to use children as a positive example, and to spend precious time with them. But children were not ancillary to His mission. They were an integral part of it.

Regardless of the enterprise you are leading, your primary question should always be, "How does what we do affect children?" This should be a leadership question because it is right, because it follows Jesus' teaching and example, and because dealing with it will, in very practical and tangible ways, contribute to your success.

Consider the children of those involved in your undertaking. How will your schedules, what you ask of the people involved, impact the lives of their children and yours? How can you be a positive influence on, not only your own children, but on children at large?

This is one of our Lord's most powerful leadership principles. Jesus loved the little children. And so should we.

Is This Speaking to You?

What's keeping you from giving your best to your children? And is it worth the price you're paying to keep it there?

WHO KNOWS?

Perhaps the best thing you can know is that you can't know everything–but that you serve a living God who does.

THE WORD FOR THE DAY

MOST OF US CAN BE REALLY GOOD AT ONLY A FEW THINGS. TRYING TO DO TOO MUCH CAN ONLY DILUTE AND WEAKEN YOUR STRENGTHS.

NEVER BE AFRAID TO SAY "I DON'T KNOW."

AS A CHRISTIAN, YOU CAN REST IN THE FACT THAT THE HOLY SPIRIT IN YOU CAN BUBBLE UP ETERNAL WISDOM AT A MOMENT'S NOTICE—RIGHT WHEN YOU NEED IT.

JUST BECAUSE YOUR PLAN DOESN'T RECEIVE IMMEDIATE CONSENSUS DOESN'T NECESSARILY MEAN YOU'RE WRONG. GIVE IDEAS TIME TO GROW AND DEVELOP.

1 CORINTHIANS 2:1-7, 9-10A

When I came to you, brothers, I did not come with eloquence or superior wisdom as I proclaimed to you the testimony about God.

For I resolved to know nothing while I was with you except Jesus Christ and him crucified. I came to you in weakness and fear, and with much trembling.

My message and my preaching were not with wise and persuasive words, but with a demonstration of the Spirit's power, so that your faith might not rest on men's wisdom, but on God's power.

We do, however, speak a message of wisdom among the mature, but not the wisdom of this age or of the rulers of this age, who are coming to nothing.

No, we speak of God's secret wisdom, a wisdom that has been hidden and that God destined for our glory before time began. . . . as it is written: "No eye has seen, no ear has heard, no mind has conceived what God has prepared for those who love him"–but God has revealed it to us by his Spirit.

LEADERSHIP PRINCIPLE NUMBER 28

LEADERS REALIZE THEY CAN'T KNOW EVERYTHING ABOUT EVERYTHING.

According to an old baseball cliché, you win some, you lose some, and some get rained out.

Every leader would like to win them all, but this is impossible. After all the marketing plans are made and the strategy is set, no one truly knows what will happen in the marketplace.

But leaders who can't handle rejection, defeat, delays, and setbacks don't last. Leaders who have to win every time are short-lived with limited success. Leaders must believe that if they sow good seed, some will fall on good soil. Some will produce good things. Even though you may not see good results immediately or even in your lifetime, Jesus teaches us that good seed will produce good fruit. We can't be discouraged by a lack of response. We must trust God to bring about the harvest in His own time and His own way.

It is important, though, to remember the rainout principle–situations that are neither won nor lost, but need to be rescheduled for a more opportune time, and should not be written off or forgotten. A time will come for them. A good leader understands this and plans accordingly.

Is This Speaking to You?

Questions are allowed. Ask them often. But ultimately, you must take action using the best information you have.

PEACE OF HIS MIND

Trusting God to accomplish His will through your work makes you no less responsible, just a lot less irritable.

THE WORD FOR THE DAY

YOU MAY HAVE LONELY DECISIONS TO MAKE, BUT YOU HAVE "A FRIEND WHO STICKS CLOSER THAN A BROTHER" (PROVERBS 18:24).

RELAX—GOD IS ALWAYS ON THE JOB.

PEACE OF MIND DOES NOT COME FROM DOING EVERYTHING PERFECTLY, BUT FROM TRUSTING GOD TO WORK THROUGH YOU.

PEACE IS NOT THE ABSENCE OF CONFLICT, BUT THE ABILITY TO STAY AT REST AMID CONFLICT.

GOD PROMISES PEACE THAT "TRANSCENDS ALL UNDERSTANDING" (PHILIPPIANS 4:7)

ISAIAH 40:27-31
PSALM 37:39-40

Why do you say, O Jacob, and complain, O Israel, "My way is hidden from the LORD; my cause is disregarded by my God"?

Do you not know? Have you not heard? The LORD is the everlasting God, the Creator of the ends of the earth. He will not grow tired or weary, and his understanding no one can fathom.

He gives strength to the weary and increases the power of the weak.

Even youths grow tired and weary, and young men stumble and fall; but those who hope in the LORD will renew their strength. They will soar on wings like eagles; they will run and not grow weary, they will walk and not be faint. . . .

The salvation of the righteous comes from the LORD; he is their stronghold in time of trouble.

The LORD helps them and delivers them; he delivers them from the wicked and saves them, because they take refuge in him.

LEADERSHIP PRINCIPLE NUMBER 29

TRUSTING GOD RESULTS IN PEACE OF MIND.

There is no substitute for peace of mind. And there is nowhere to find it except in relationship with Jesus Christ.

Too often in business, people tend to think that Christian faith is not applicable to what they do on a day-to-day basis. They think that Christianity is a Sunday morning component of life, but totally unrelated from the rest of their week.

But I dare you to ask one business executive, organizational leader, or anyone in a position of authority what they would give to have peace of mind, a calmness in their soul, the ability to lay down their worries at the end of the day and sleep soundly through the night. They'd give just about anything to know that kind of peace.

But it only comes through Jesus Christ. Even then it's not easy. Even as a Christian, you'll find it hard to release your cares into His custody and trust Him to give you wisdom and perspective. But I guarantee you, you'll find it nowhere else. Christian faith not only brings the wisdom of the ages within reach, it brings the peace of God into your heart. And you can rest in that.

Is This Speaking to You?

Feeling the weight of the world on your shoulders? Trust your troubles to One who's worth His weight in wisdom.

CHURCH SERVICE

The church may already be your arena of leadership. But we all have a responsibility to pull our weight in this family.

THE WORD FOR THE DAY

FAITHFULNESS IN YOUR CHURCH LIFE WILL VALIDATE YOUR PUBLIC LIFE.

THE BIBLE INDICATES THAT THOSE WITH GREATER RESPONSIBILITIES ARE HELD TO A HIGHER LEVEL OF ACCOUNTABILITY. DON'T COMPARE YOUR CONTRIBUTIONS WITH OTHERS.

"LET US CONSIDER . . . ONE ANOTHER." ONE OF THE MAIN REASONS WE NEED OUR CHURCH IS TO TAKE OUR ATTENTION OFF OUR OWN NEEDS.

LEADERSHIP MAY COME EASY TO YOU, BUT IT DOESN'T TO EVERYONE. ARE YOU LETTING GOD USE YOUR LEADERSHIP GIFT—AND ALL YOUR GIFTS—IN MINISTRY?

HEBREWS 10:19-25
1 CORINTHIANS 12:12

Therefore, brothers, since we have confidence to enter the Most Holy Place by the blood of Jesus, by a new and living way opened for us through the curtain, that is, his body, and since we have a great priest over the house of God, let us draw near to God with a sincere heart in full assurance of faith, having our hearts sprinkled to cleanse us from a guilty conscience and having our bodies washed with pure water.

Let us hold unswervingly to the hope we profess, for he who promised is faithful.

And let us consider how we may spur one another on towards love and good deeds.

Let us not give up meeting together, as some are in the habit of doing, but let us encourage one another–and all the more as you see the Day approaching. . . .

The body is a unit, though it is made up of many parts; and though all its parts are many, they form one body. So it is with Christ.

LEADERSHIP PRINCIPLE NUMBER 30

CHRISTIAN LEADERS SHOULD SET ASIDE TIME FOR CHURCH AND PERSONAL MINISTRY.

The world does not understand Christian fellowship, but we need to be sure we do. We need to place a high value on it and make sure we both give and receive it. Without regular, meaningful relationships with other Christians, we can never live the joyful, kingdom-building life God intends for us.

Many of your associates may be people who either do not understand your Christian faith or are openly antagonistic toward it. And much of your time may be spent on topics and situations that are far removed from the classic themes of our faith. But if you do not program Christian fellowship into your life, you will soon begin to think and act like those colleagues who are not followers of Jesus. I have seen it happen, and I know that if I am not careful, it will happen to me.

As churches become bigger and more professional, it is becoming easier to be an anonymous believer who slips into his seat on Sunday and then leaves without speaking to anyone or being spoken to. But your spiritual survival in the midst of career obligations could very well depend on the quality of Christian fellowship you have.

Is This Speaking to You?

When you write out your tithe check this week, ask yourself whether you've tithed your time *to the Lord, as well.*

WORK YOUR PLAN

The time you spend in putting legs, arms, and feet on your vision will be the best investment you make as a leader.

THE WORD FOR THE DAY

NEHEMIAH GOT HIS BIG BREAK BECAUSE HE WAS READY WITH AN ANSWER TO THE KING'S OFFHAND QUESTION.

SEVEN OTHER TIMES THE BIBLE MENTIONS NEHEMIAH'S PRAYING. THAT'S WHERE PLANNING SHOULD START.

HE WASN'T AFRAID TO ASK FOR EVEN MORE THAN HE REALLY EXPECTED TO GET.

PART OF NEHEMIAH'S PLAN WAS TO PLAN FOR OPPOSITION.

ABOVE ALL, HE KNEW THAT THE SUCCESS OF HIS UNDERTAKING DEPENDED TOTALLY ON GOD.

NEHEMIAH 2:4-8

The king said to me, "What is it you want?" Then I prayed to the God of heaven, and I answered the king, "If it pleases the king and if your servant has found favor in his sight, let him send me to the city in Judah where my fathers are buried so that I can rebuild it."

Then the king, with the queen sitting beside him, asked me, "How long will your journey take, and when will you get back?" It pleased the king to send me; so I set a time.

I also said to him, "If it pleases the king, may I have letters to the governors of Trans-Euphrates, so that they will provide me safe-conduct until I arrive in Judah?

"And may I have a letter to Asaph, keeper of the king's forest, so he will give me timber to make beams for the gates of the citadel by the temple and for the city wall and for the residence I will occupy?" And because the gracious hand of my God was upon me, the king granted my requests.

LEADERSHIP PRINCIPLE NUMBER 31

PROPER PLANNING CAN HELP YOU AVOID MOST OF YOUR MISTAKES.

Leaders react to unexpected opportunities and obstacles, enabling them to maximize unanticipated situations. But this does not mean they do not plan. Visionary leadership requires both a long-range view of opportunities and short-range plans to advance to the next level. Measure your leadership by this. Do you have the ultimate goal clearly in mind? Do you know how to move to the next step?

Is God interested in the details? Read Exodus 25-40 and study God's extremely detailed instructions for the construction of the tabernacle. He provides a blueprint any architect would admire. God cares about the details, and so should we.

Jesus' master plan is the most brilliant and awe-inspiring one ever conceived. He repeatedly demonstrated His leadership abilities through the precision of His planning. In even the seemingly small things, He led by planning–from the colt ready for His triumphal entry into Jerusalem to an upper room ready for the Last Supper. He made things happen by planning.

Follow His perfect example. Be a leader. Be a planner.

Is This Speaking to You?

Before you take another step in the wrong direction, back up to where you started. And start off again with a plan.

SINGLE MINDED

It's only when you truly know what your driving purpose is that you can steer your life in the direction God desires.

THE WORD FOR THE DAY

JESUS KNEW EXACTLY WHO HE WAS. THAT FACT MADE HIM ABLE TO ORDER HIS EARTHLY LIFE BENEATH HIS PURPOSE AND PRIORITIES.

OTHERS MAY NOT ALWAYS UNDERSTAND WHY YOU DO WHAT YOU DO, WHY YOU MUST SOMETIMES SAY NO TO THE FUN AND FLEETING.

IT IS HELPFUL AT TIMES TO PUT YOUR PRIORITIES ON PAPER, AND TO REFER TO THEM DOWN THE ROAD TO SEE IF YOU'RE STAYING ON TRACK.

ARE YOUR LIFE'S GOALS DEFINED BY YOUR RELATIONSHIP WITH JESUS? IF NOT, YOU SHOULD MAKE NEW ONES.

JOHN 8:13-14, 25-29

The Pharisees challenged him, "Here you are, appearing as your own witness; your testimony is not valid."

Jesus answered, "Even if I testify on my own behalf, my testimony is valid, for I know where I came from and where I am going. But you have no idea where I come from or where I am going. . . .

"Who are you?" they asked. "Just what I have been claiming all along," Jesus replied. "I have much to say in judgment of you. But he who sent me is reliable, and what I have heard from him I tell the world."

They did not understand that he was telling them about his Father.

So Jesus said, "When you have lifted up the Son of Man, then you will know that I am the one I claim to be and that I do nothing on my own but speak just what the Father has taught me.

"The one who sent me is with me; he has not left me alone, for I always do what pleases him."

LEADERSHIP PRINCIPLE NUMBER 32

KNOW WHAT YOUR PURPOSE IS, AND MAKE SURE YOUR ACTIVITIES LINE UP UNDERNEATH IT.

God has specific plans for each of us, and we must do our best to determine what they are and submit to them. When we fail to do this, less than God's best often transpires. For example, a very gifted teacher at a Christian college–a man *called* to teach–was railroaded into the college presidency by well-meaning colleagues, resulting in trauma, hard feelings, and disappointment on all sides. Gifts in one area, such as leadership abilities, are not transferable.

Never let someone else determine God's will for your life. No one else can understand God's unique call on your life as clearly as you. You can waste so many years trying in vain to please others when you would have been far more productive living as God designed you to live. This doesn't mean we go off half-cocked or without advice. But in the end, each one of us must face God individually.

When we consider taking positions of leadership, we need to seek God's affirmation. We may not hear an audible voice from heaven, but we can know that we are acting within God's will for our lives.

Is This Speaking to You?

Do you have a feel for God's will? Do you know where you're going? Will you know it when you get there?

OK, WHAT'S NEXT?

Adversity is a main course in the leader's diet. And the best way to swallow it is to eat everything that's on your plate.

THE WORD FOR THE DAY

"BUT JONAH RAN AWAY FROM THE LORD." RUNNING FROM YOUR PROBLEMS ONLY MAKES THEM GROW STRONGER.

TRY TACKLING YOUR HARDEST TASKS FIRST, RATHER THAN DREADING THEM ALL DAY.

IF YOUR MAIN SOURCE OF ADVERSITY IS OTHER PEOPLE, LEARN THE FINE ART OF BEING GENTLE BUT DIRECT, CALM BUT CLEAR. AS HARD AS IT IS NOW, IT WILL ONLY GET WORSE IF YOU LET THINGS GO.

GOD GAVE JONAH A SECOND CHANCE. HE KNOWS THIS IS A TOUGH ONE. JUST KEEP TRYING.

JONAH 1:1-4, 10, 11B, 15, 17

The word of the LORD came to Jonah son of Amittai: "Go to the great city of Nineveh and preach against it, because its wickedness has come up before me."

But Jonah ran away from the LORD and headed for Tarshish. He went down to Joppa, where he found a ship bound for that port. After paying the fare, he went aboard and sailed for Tarshish to flee from the LORD.

Then the LORD sent a great wind on the sea, and such a violent storm arose that the ship threatened to break up.

This terrified them and they asked, "What have you done?" (They knew he was running away from the LORD, because he had already told them so.) . . . So they asked him, "What should we do to you to make the sea calm down for us?" . . .

Then they took Jonah and threw him overboard, and the raging sea grew calm. . . .

But the LORD provided a great fish to swallow Jonah, and Jonah was inside the fish three days and three nights.

LEADERSHIP PRINCIPLE NUMBER 33

LEADERS SHOULD NOT SEEK ADVERSITY, BUT SHOULDN'T RUN FROM IT EITHER.

I have been associated in business with people who seek strife, who are not happy unless there is current controversy, and who will generate dispute if none arises naturally. That kind of attitude is antithetical to God's way for us. We should see peace as a goal and strive for it. That doesn't mean Christians should be passive, rolling over anytime someone comes along with a lawsuit. We need to be firm in our convictions and fight fairly and diligently to defend ourselves. But I admire those individuals who can be embroiled in a legal action, yet maintain a beautiful sense of calm and dignity.

If someone wrongs you and legal action seems necessary, fight strongly and fairly with the power that comes from righteousness. Honor God through every step, and He will honor you. And if you are served papers for something you have done or haven't done, tap into that same source of power. Regardless of the outcome in terms of our country's legal system, you will emerge a true winner. You will sleep soundly at night and be able to face the next day with the confidence that comes from obeying God.

Is This Speaking to You?

You may have tried everything you know to conquer a nagging problem. Have you asked God for an action plan?

TALKING POINTS

Communication can be talking, listening, whatever. But one thing's for sure. Communication better be happening.

THE WORD FOR THE DAY

ONE OF THE BIGGEST OBSTACLES TO SUCCESSFUL COMMUNICATION IS NOT KNOWING EXACTLY WHAT YOU'RE TRYING TO SAY. DON'T EXPECT OTHERS TO UNDERSTAND SOMETHING YOU DON'T QUITE UNDERSTAND YOURSELF.

WHAT MAY SEEM LIKE A LACK OF EFFORT MAY REALLY BE A LACK OF CONFIDENCE. THE DISCIPLES CERTAINLY DIDN'T FEEL UP TO THEIR TASK, BUT JESUS INSTILLED CONFIDENCE IN THEM.

ARE YOU COMMUNICATING CLEAR GOALS AND MEASURABLE REWARDS? PEOPLE LIKE TO SEE THAT WHAT THEY'RE DOING IS MAKING A DIFFERENCE.

LUKE 9:1-6, 10-11

When Jesus had called the Twelve together, he gave them power and authority to drive out all demons and to cure diseases, and he sent them out to preach the kingdom of God and to heal the sick.

He told them: "Take nothing for the journey–no staff, no bag, no bread, no money, no extra tunic. Whatever house you enter, stay there until you leave that town. If people do not welcome you, shake the dust off your feet when you leave their town, as a testimony against them."

So they set out and went from village to village, preaching the gospel and healing people everywhere. . . .

When the apostles returned, they reported to Jesus what they had done. Then he took them with him and they withdrew by themselves to a town called Bethsaida, but the crowds learned about it and followed him. He welcomed them and spoke to them about the kingdom of God, and healed those who needed healing.

LEADERSHIP PRINCIPLE NUMBER 34

EFFECTIVE LEADERS KEEP THEIR LINES OF COMMUNICATION OPEN, CLEAR, AND HONEST.

As you lead, the idea to have your people report to you in written form may seem like a good one. You can peruse the reports as you have the time to do so, you have a written record of your workers' activities, and you are able to jot appropriate notes back–all very neat and orderly. But so much is lost.

A wise leader does not rely solely on notes and memos to communicate with those he leads. He takes time to "lead by walking around," to use a Tom Peters phrase. He sees and is seen by those doing the work, so that team members can receive regular personal time with and easy access to their leader whenever necessary.

When Jesus' disciples returned from the successful mission Jesus had sent them on–one which enabled them to practice many of the things He had told them–can you imagine how eager they were to report to Him? This must have been a joyful, energizing time.

Don't waste valuable opportunities to lead by saying, "Just send me a note on that." Take Jesus' lead. Gather your people around you and let them tell you "all they [have] done and taught."

Is This Speaking to You?

____

____

____

____

____

____

____

____

____

____

____

____

____

____

____

____

____

____

____

____

____

____

When problems arise between you and others under your authority, ask yourself a question: Am I communicating?

DO UNTO OTHERS

*There's not a decision you'll make today that can't be run through the Golden Rule filter. What **would** Jesus do?*

THE WORD FOR THE DAY

THE HARDEST THINGS TO DO AND THE EASIEST THINGS TO FORGET ARE SOMETIMES THE SIMPLEST AND MOST BASIC.

LETTING BIBLICAL PRINCIPLES GUIDE YOUR LEADERSHIP TASKS GIVES YOU EXAMPLES TO SHARE WITH OTHERS ABOUT HOW GOD'S WORD APPLIES TO DAILY LIFE.

JESUS TOOK TIME TO HEAR AND ENCOURAGE THIS ONE WHO WAS TRULY SEEKING HIM. HE KNOWS YOUR HEART.

YOU NEED NO OTHER EXPLANATION THAN THIS FOR ONE OF YOUR LEADERSHIP ACTIONS: "IT'S A GOLDEN RULE THING."

MARK 12:28-34A

One of the teachers of the law came and heard them debating. Noticing that Jesus had given them a good answer, he asked him, "Of all the commandments, which is the most important?"

"The most important one," answered Jesus, "is this: 'Hear, O Israel, the Lord our God, the Lord is one. Love the Lord your God with all your heart and with all your soul and with all your mind and with all your strength.'

The second is this: 'Love your neighbor as yourself.' There is no commandment greater than these."

"Well said, teacher," the man replied. "You are right in saying that God is one and there is no other but him. To love him with all your heart, with all your understanding and with all your strength, and to love your neighbor as yourself is more important than all burnt offerings and sacrifices."

When Jesus saw that he had answered wisely, he said to him, "You are not far from the kingdom of God."

LEADERSHIP PRINCIPLE NUMBER 35

DO TO OTHERS AS YOU WOULD HAVE THEM DO TO YOU.

The general decline in basic civility and personal integrity, as lamentable as it is, presents a wonderful opportunity for modern Christians–particularly for Christian businessmen. Christians can have a very positive impact by learning to exercise what were once just ordinary standards of courtesy toward those with whom we do business. We can literally "shine like stars," to use the beautiful phrase from Philippians, as our behavior contrasts so vividly with that of other people in business.

My business and nonbusiness activities bring me into contact with a wide variety of people, from the most secular to the most Christian. I am sorry to say that there is very little difference between the business manners of Christians and non-Christians. In fact, I must admit that, overall, non-Christians may perform better. Yet if any group should be concerned about relating positively and politely to those around them, sending signals of caring commitment to quality relationships, it should be Christians in business. There is a tremendous need for Christians to stand out and make a difference.

Is This Speaking to You?

What rules are defining your daily choices? Try putting on paper the godly guidelines that you want driving you.

A SACRED TRUST

The demands of leadership can get over your head in a hurry. But there's one Person who's never overwhelmed.

THE WORD FOR THE DAY

DAVID MADE HIS MISTAKES, BUT HE WAS ALWAYS WILLING TO GET UP AND PUT HIS TRUST IN THE LORD . . . AGAIN.

BE LISTENING FOR GOD'S WISDOM AT ANY HOUR OF THE DAY, FOR "EVEN AT NIGHT MY HEART INSTRUCTS ME."

GOD IS NOT JUST A QUIET TIME COMPANION BUT THE "RIGHT HAND" MAN OF THE CHRISTIAN.

JOB SECURITY? GOD'S PLAN FOR YOU IS MUCH MORE SECURE THAN THAT.

TRUSTING GOD ALLOWS YOU TO SEE YOUR DAILY DECISIONS FROM AN ETERNAL PERSPECTIVE.

PSALM 16:1-2, 5-11

Keep me safe, O God, for in you I take refuge.

I said to the LORD, "You are my Lord; apart from you I have no good thing. . . ."

LORD, you have assigned me my portion and my cup; you have made my lot secure.

The boundary lines have fallen for me in pleasant places; surely I have a delightful inheritance.

I will praise the LORD, who counsels me; even at night my heart instructs me.

I have set the LORD always before me. Because he is at my right hand, I shall not be shaken.

Therefore my heart is glad and my tongue rejoices; my body also will rest secure, because you will not abandon me to the grave, nor will you let your Holy One see decay.

You have made known to me the path of life; you will fill me with joy in your presence, with eternal pleasures at your right hand.

For every challenge in business, there is the possibility that you will mess it up. For every opportunity that comes your way, there is the possibility that it will slip through your fingers. But for every situation you face in your leadership role, there is a new chance for you to exercise your total trust in God and to see it make a difference in the way you handle your work.

LEADERSHIP PRINCIPLE NUMBER 36

SUCCESSFUL LEADERS ARE ABLE TO LEAN THE FULL WEIGHT OF THEIR RESPONSIBILITY ON GOD'S ABILITY.

I wish I could recall all the times I've looked into the face of an impossible situation, one that had so many twists and angles and moving parts, the potential for failure seemed almost a foregone conclusion. Too many things could go wrong. Unfortunately, I have far too often failed to fully trust that God could help me through difficulties like these. But every time that I have sincerely trusted in Him, He has either caused me to succeed or brought about an even better opportunity out of the midst of defeat.

That's simply the way He works with His people. Why are we so hardheaded about forcing our own way when God wants to lead us in the perfect way? Learn the secret of trust in God, and you will save yourself many a mistake.

Is This Speaking to You?

When you want something to be handled right, you're always better off leaving it in God's hands than in yours.

DAY THIRTY-SEVEN

THE ONE YOU LOVE

You have promised your best to your leadership responsibility. But you have promised your life to your wife.

THE WORD FOR THE DAY

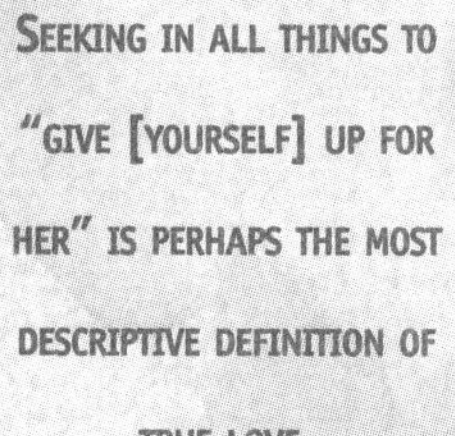

PEOPLE OBVIOUSLY PLACE THEIR CONFIDENCE IN YOU. BUT NO ONE'S PRAISE SHOULD BE AS SWEET IN YOUR EARS AS YOUR OWN WIFE'S.

SEEKING IN ALL THINGS TO "GIVE [YOURSELF] UP FOR HER" IS PERHAPS THE MOST DESCRIPTIVE DEFINITION OF TRUE LOVE.

THE BEST MARRIAGE IS THE ONE WHERE HUSBAND AND WIFE ARE BOTH SERVING EACH OTHER.

HOME AND FAMILY CAN BECOME THE FIRST THINGS TO FALL OFF YOUR PRIORITY LIST. BUT YOUR GREATEST REWARD IN LIFE WILL COME FROM WHAT YOU ACCOMPLISH THERE.

EPHESIANS 5:25-32

Husbands, love your wives, just as Christ loved the church and gave himself up for her to make her holy, cleansing her by the washing with water through the word, and to present her to himself as a radiant church, without stain or wrinkle or any other blemish, but holy and blameless.

In this same way, husbands ought to love their wives as their own bodies. He who loves his wife loves himself.

After all, no one ever hated his own body, but he feeds and cares for it, just as Christ does the church–for we are members of his body.

"For this reason a man will leave his father and mother and be united to his wife, and the two will become one flesh."

This is a profound mystery–but I am talking about Christ and the church.

However, each one of you also must love his wife as he loves himself, and the wife must respect her husband.

LEADERSHIP PRINCIPLE NUMBER 37

YOUR SPOUSE DESERVES YOUR LOVE, TIME, AND ATTENTION.

There is a very real sense in which a Christian marriage is a window in time through which others catch a glimpse of eternity. We are like actors on a stage with the whole world watching. Our marriage is our starring role. When a husband plays his part well, the audience sees something deeper. They see Christ and the church. That's the way God set it up, which is why a Christian marriage either draws people to Christ or drives them farther away.

Here's some exciting news. You are a missionary to your office, and your marriage is your message. You don't have to preach a sermon. Your lifetime commitment to your wife is a visible sermon that people see every day.

How can you show God's love to others? Let them see it in your marriage. It's more effective than a hundred tracts or two hundred Scripture verses. People may doubt the things you say, but they cannot deny the reality of a truly Christian marriage.

Marriage matters to God, and it ought to matter to you. When leaders keep their vows, it becomes easier for followers to keep their promises.

Is This Speaking to You?

Do something special for your wife today. It will remind her of your love, and remind you to love her.

WHO? ME?

If you're feeling outmatched by a certain job or challenge, you're probably right where God wants you to be.

THE WORD FOR THE DAY

WHERE GOD GUIDES, GOD PROVIDES. MOSES, LIKE US, HAD ONLY ONE RESPONSIBILITY IN THIS SITUATION: TO OBEY.

GOD'S HEARD ALL YOUR EXCUSES BEFORE. IF HE HAS PLACED YOU IN A CERTAIN FIELD OF RESPONSIBILITY, HE WILL WORK THROUGH YOU.

UNSURE ABOUT WHETHER THIS TASK IS EVEN GOD'S WILL FOR YOU? STUDY THE WORD, SEEK WISE COUNSEL, AND TRUST GOD TO TURN EVEN YOUR MISTAKES INTO SUCCESSES.

"FOR WHEN I AM WEAK, THEN I AM STRONG" (2 CORINTHIANS 12:10).

EXODUS 3:10-12A, 13, 4:1, 10-13

"I am sending you to Pharaoh to bring my people the Israelites out of Egypt."

But Moses said to God, "Who am I, that I should go to Pharaoh and bring the Israelites out of Egypt?" And God said, "I will be with you. . . ."

Moses said to God, "Suppose I go to the Israelites and say to them, 'The God of your fathers has sent me to you,' and they ask me, 'What is his name?' Then what shall I tell them? . . . What if they do not believe me or listen to me and say, 'The LORD did not appear to you'?" . . . O Lord, I have never been eloquent, neither in the past nor since you have spoken to your servant. I am slow of speech and tongue."

The LORD said to him, "Who gave man his mouth? Who makes him deaf or mute? Who gives him sight or makes him blind? Is it not I, the LORD?

"Now go; I will help you speak and will teach you what to say."

But Moses said, "O Lord, please send someone else to do it."

LEADERSHIP PRINCIPLE NUMBER 38

THE CURE FOR INSECURITY IS BELIEF IN GOD'S MISSION AND BELIEF IN GOD'S HELP.

Hardly a day goes by but that I have to make a decision. On a good day, the decisions are pretty easy. I usually have about three of those good days a year. The rest of the time, the decisions are tough. Make the right call, and my company makes some money. Make the wrong one, and we lose bundles.

Then there are the real tough ones–decisions involving people. Make the right call, and no one gets hurt. Make the wrong one, and someone's out of a job, Or worse. Those are the ones that keep me awake at night.

Fortunately, every believer has a resource to help with those decisions: the very heart and mind of God. Unfortunately, we don't always avail ourselves of this opportunity. Frankly, it sometimes seems trite to go to the Lord with a decision about a business deal. He's got better things to do, we tell ourselves. And then we wonder why we're in hot water when a tough call we made goes against us. But if we take God at His word, we realize that He does care about the things that are important to us, and offers to guide us with His wisdom. All we have to do is ask.

Is This Speaking to You?

Insecurities are God's way of reminding you Who's in charge here. Trust His strength to keep you afloat.

GLORY TO GOD

Oh, the warm rush of pride when people pour on the praise. But oh, how much sweeter, when it goes to God instead.

THE WORD FOR THE DAY

NEVER BELIEVE YOUR WORK IS AS GREAT AS PEOPLE SAY IT IS, NOR AS BAD AS PEOPLE SAY IT IS.

SHOW THE DOOR TO EVERY PROUD THOUGHT THAT ENTERS YOUR HEAD. IT'S SATAN'S FAVORITE WAY IN. YOU'LL HAVE TO LEAN ON GOD HARD TO KEEP HIM OUT.

SOMETIMES OUR SPIRITUAL WORDS JUST MAKE US SOUND MORE SPIRITUAL. IS GOD GETTING THE GLORY IN YOUR HEART?

"NOT TO US, O LORD, NOT TO US BUT TO YOUR NAME BE THE GLORY, BECAUSE OF YOUR LOVE AND FAITHFULNESS" (PSALM 115:1).

PSALM 66:5, 8-12, 16-20

Come and see what God has done, how awesome his works on man's behalf. . . .

Praise our God, O peoples, let the sound of his praise be heard; he has preserved our lives and kept our feet from slipping.

For you, O God, tested us; you refined us like silver. You brought us into prison and laid burdens on our backs.

You let men ride over our heads; we went through fire and water, but you brought us to a place of abundance. . . .

Come and listen, all you who fear God; let me tell you what he has done for me.

I cried out to him with my mouth; his praise was on my tongue.

If I had cherished sin in my heart, the Lord would not have listened; but God has surely listened and heard my voice in prayer.

Praise be to God, who has not rejected my prayer or withheld his love from me!

BRINER NOTES

LEADERSHIP PRINCIPLE NUMBER 39

GENUINE LEADERS GIVE GOD THE CREDIT FOR THEIR TALENTS AND SUCCESSES.

There is really no such thing as a self-made man. No matter how high you have been able to climb, from no matter how low a starting point you came from, you stand on the tall shoulders of other people who have helped you along the way–and the even taller shoulders of God, who is truly the source behind every step in your advancement.

The story of the Israelites in the Old Testament is a story of remembrance and forgetfulness. So often, God spoke through His prophets to remind them how easy it is to forget, how quickly the lull of a smooth road can cause a person's dependence on God to seem a distant, unnecessary annoyance. Moses urged them to "be careful, and watch yourselves closely so that you do not forget the things your eyes have seen or let them slip from your heart" (Deut. 4:9).

When people are bragging on you, when your work is drawing attention, those are the times when you can easily forget all He has provided to get you where you are. Don't let yourself forget the source of your strength. Give God the glory that people give to you.

Is This Speaking to You?

____

____

____

____

____

____

____

____

____

____

____

____

____

____

____

____

____

____

____

____

____

____

Your accolades are not yours to be taken personally, but are your own opportunities to give personal thanks to God.

REST FOR THE WEARY

From one vantage point, rest can look like doing nothing. But in reality, it's one of the most useful things you can do.

THE WORD FOR THE DAY

GOD, OF COURSE, HAD NO NEED TO REST. "INDEED, HE WHO WATCHES OVER ISRAEL WILL NEITHER SLUMBER NOR SLEEP" (PSALM 121:4).

HIS RESTING WAS AN EXAMPLE TO US, WHICH HE LATER ISSUED AS COMMANDMENT #4, TEACHING US TO INCLUDE REST IN OUR ROUTINE.

"KEEPING IT HOLY" MEANS TO *SEPARATE* OR *SET APART* THE SABBATH FROM NORMAL EVERYDAY ACTIONS.

THE NEW TESTAMENT CALLS OUR SALVATION A "SABBATH-REST" FROM OUR LABORS (HEBREWS 4:10).

GENESIS 1:31-2:2
EXODUS 20:8-11

God saw all that he had made, and it was very good. And there was evening, and there was morning—the sixth day.

Thus the heavens and the earth were completed in all their vast array.

By the seventh day God had finished the work he had been doing; so on the seventh day he rested from all his work. . . .

"Remember the Sabbath day by keeping it holy.

"Six days you shall labor and do all your work, but the seventh day is a Sabbath to the LORD your God. On it you shall not do any work, neither you, nor your son or daughter, nor your manservant or maidservant, nor your animals, nor the alien within your gates.

"For in six days the LORD made the heavens and the earth, the sea, and all that is in them, but he rested on the seventh day. Therefore the LORD blessed the Sabbath day and made it holy."

LEADERSHIP PRINCIPLE NUMBER 40

MAKE YOURSELF TAKE TIME TO REST AND REFRESH.

Even with all that Jesus had to accomplish during His short stay on earth, He still took plenty of time off. He made sure He had time alone for prayer and reflection. He got His sleep. There were times when everyone else was awake but Jesus was sleeping.

As always, He is a great example for us. It may seem politically savvy and the macho thing to be thought of as a guy always on the go, never resting, never getting away. But a well-rested executive always accomplishes more than a tired, stressed-out executive. Take your vacations. Real vacations. Ones in which you truly do get away from the office. To remove even the temptation to check in, you might even consider going to places where there are no phones. You will come back refreshed, energized, and ready to get back into the action with gusto.

And remember, as important as it is for you to get away, it is just as important for your subordinates to get away. A smart executive will make sure that his employees, in their zeal to please, to advance, or to make just one more deal, don't drive themselves so hard that they have a flame-out.

Is This Speaking to You?

Life can keep your mind at work around the clock. You owe it to yourself to shut down for a little while.

YOUR RESPONSIBILITY

While others are blaming someone else or making excuses, a quality leader is telling the accusers to start with him.

THE WORD FOR THE DAY

WHEN OTHERS POINT FINGERS AND QUESTION YOUR ABILITY, QUIETLY REMEMBER HOW LITTLE THEY KNOW ABOUT HOW MUCH YOU DO.

PAUL'S LEADERSHIP IN THE CHURCH CAUSED HIM TO BECOME "ITS SERVANT." YOUR LEADERSHIP WILL DO NO LESS.

YOUR RESPONSIBILITIES COULD KEEP YOU UP ALL NIGHT EVERY NIGHT IF YOU LET THEM. YOU MUST ALLOW GOD TO CARRY YOUR CONCERNS.

ASK GOD TO LET OTHERS SEE, NOT YOUR OWN CAPABILITIES, BUT "HIS ENERGY, WHICH SO POWERFULLY WORKS" IN YOU.

COLOSSIANS 1:24–2:1

Now I rejoice in what was suffered for you, and I fill up in my flesh what is still lacking in regard to Christ's afflictions, for the sake of his body, which is the church.

I have become its servant by the commission God gave me to present to you the word of God in its fullness–the mystery that has been kept hidden for ages and generations, but is now disclosed to the saints.

To them God has chosen to make known among the Gentiles the glorious riches of this mystery, which is Christ in you, the hope of glory.

We proclaim him, admonishing and teaching everyone with all wisdom, so that we may present everyone perfect in Christ.

To this end I labor, struggling with all his energy, which so powerfully works in me.

I want you to know how much I am struggling for you. . . .

LEADERSHIP PRINCIPLE NUMBER 41

LEADERS TAKE RESPONSIBILITY FOR WHAT HAPPENS UNDER THEIR WATCH.

When outsiders criticize your staff, they are indirectly criticizing you. So when you stand up for your people, you are building loyalty and camaraderie while also defending yourself.

Jesus always defended His disciples. When the Pharisees criticized them, He knew that He was the ultimate target of their scorn. It must have engendered a great feeling among the disciples to have the Master come to their defense and take the brunt of the verbal attack.

When your people are doing their best, when they are honest in their efforts to serve you and the company, stand up for them in the face of outside criticism. When you cannot defend them and their performance against outside attack, either you or they need to move on.

This does not mean you should deny their mistakes. But it is possible to acknowledge an honest error without denigrating the person unfortunate enough to have made one. "That was a mistake we all participated in. You just happened to be the one who was on the front line when it happened." That's the kind of statement that serves everyone well.

Is This Speaking to You?

Responsibility grows on you. As you practice it more faithfully today, you'll be even more ready for tomorrow.

I'M NOT SURPRISED

You'll meet lots of obstacles and opposition on the path of leadership. But anything worth doing is worth fighting for.

THE WORD FOR THE DAY

SUCCESS IN A WORTHY ENDEAVOR WILL STIR UP OPPOSITION. EFFECTIVE LEADERS COUNTER WITH POSITIVE WORDS AND PRODUCTIVE ACTION.

NEHEMIAH PRAYED TO GOD *AND* POSTED A GUARD. LEADERS PRAY, BUT LEADERS ALSO ACT.

REALISTIC PLANNING TAKES ADVERSITY INTO ACCOUNT.

CHALLENGES ARE MEANT TO BE PREPARED FOR AND LEARNED FROM, NOT TO BE AFRAID OF.

WHEN PEOPLE ARE LED IN A GREAT CAUSE, THEY WILL GO TO GREAT LENGTHS TO SERVE.

NEHEMIAH 4:7-9, 13-15

But when Sanballat, Tobiah, the Arabs, the Ammonites and the men of Ashdod heard that the repairs to Jerusalem's walls had gone ahead and that the gaps were being closed, they were very angry.

They all plotted together to come and fight against Jerusalem and stir up trouble against it. But we prayed to our God and posted a guard day and night to meet this threat. . . .

Therefore I stationed some of the people behind the lowest points of the wall at the exposed places, posting them by families, with their swords, spears and bows.

After I looked things over, I stood up and said to the nobles, the officials and the rest of the people, "Don't be afraid of them. Remember the Lord, who is great and awesome, and fight for your brothers, your sons and your daughters, your wives and your homes."

When our enemies heard that we were aware of their plot and that God had frustrated it, we all returned to the wall, each to his own work.

LEADERSHIP PRINCIPLE NUMBER 42

KNOW THAT OPPOSITION WILL CERTAINLY COME. BE READY FOR IT.

His professors at Harvard Business School told Fred Smith that his plan for Federal Express was interesting, but could never work. Today FedEx is a worldwide household name and a hugely profitable multi-billion dollar business. When Jim and Carol Cymbala began their involvement with the Brooklyn Tabernacle, they were meeting in a small storefront with ten people in the congregation. Many told them to give up and get "real" jobs. Today, several thousand gather each Sunday to worship at the beautiful building in downtown Brooklyn. The Tabernacle choir is world renowned, and the ministries of the Brooklyn Tabernacle touch every borough of New York City.

Nehemiah's example of prayer and action is valuable for every leader. Both are essential. Commit your undertaking to God, then do your best to make good things happen. Nehemiah also demonstrated how important it is to be an inspirational leader as well as a good tactician. Quality inspiration and quality execution in a great cause can energize followers to produce results far beyond their normal abilities. This is leadership.

Is This Speaking to You?

Listen and learn from the voice of challenge and opposition. But if you're sure you're doing right, press on through it.

A WORD OF THANKS

When you say thanks to others, you build up a lot more than their own esteem. You make yourself stand taller, too.

THE WORD FOR THE DAY

PAUL SOMETIMES COMES OFF AS A LITTLE GRUFF, BUT HE LOVED THE PEOPLE IN THESE CHURCHES LIKE A FATHER.

CAN YOU, LIKE PAUL, HONESTLY TELL THE PEOPLE YOU WORK AROUND THAT YOU'VE BEEN "MENTIONING [THEM] IN [YOUR] PRAYERS?"

"YOU KNOW WE NEVER USED FLATTERY." IT'S BETTER TO SAY NOTHING THAN TO POUR ON THE PRAISE WITHOUT MEANING IT.

GRATITUDE HAS BECOME A LOST VIRTUE IN OUR GENERATION. YOUR CHILDREN NEED TO SEE YOUR THANKFUL HEART.

1 THESSALONIANS 1:1-3, 2:5-8

Paul, Silas and Timothy, To the church of the Thessalonians in God the Father and the Lord Jesus Christ: Grace and peace to you.

We always thank God for all of you, mentioning you in our prayers.

We continually remember before our God and Father your work produced by faith, your labor prompted by love, and your endurance inspired by hope in our Lord Jesus Christ. . . .

You know we never used flattery, nor did we put on a mask to cover up greed–God is our witness.

We were not looking for praise from men, not from you or anyone else. As apostles of Christ we could have been a burden to you, but we were gentle among you, like a mother caring for her little children.

We loved you so much that we were delighted to share with you not only the gospel of God but our lives as well, because you had become so dear to us.

LEADERSHIP PRINCIPLE NUMBER 43

GOOD LEADERS REMEMBER WHAT THOSE WHO SERVE UNDER THEM HAVE DONE TO HELP.

Jack Kinder, the well known management consultant, says that anyone in business who does not write at least ten thank you letters a month is not maximizing the potential of his business. This is a powerful lesson for Christian leaders.

The Apostle Paul gives us a wonderful example of this principle. Passages like this one not only demonstrate his care and concern for people, but provide a great example for leaders in every kind of enterprise.

We need to be letter writers. We need to communicate. We need to network. We need to recognize people. We need to say thanks. Far too many people allow valuable relationships to dissipate through sheer neglect. All kinds of enterprises, particularly Christian enterprises, are hurt because the people involved do not answer their mail, return phone calls, or say thanks. Our failures in communication–timely communication–are detrimental to the cause of Christ.

As leaders, we need to appropriate the methods of the Apostle Paul as demonstrated in this passage. We need to set an example of timely, consistent, personal, caring communication.

Is This Speaking to You?

Have you taken the time to say thanks to someone lately? Go out of your way to make it a top priority today.

ROUTINE SERVICE

If the high road of leadership doesn't take you across the low road of servanthood, you need to get some new directions.

THE WORD FOR THE DAY

PERSONAL AMBITION ALWAYS OBSCURES THE MAIN PURPOSE OF THE GROUP OR ENDEAVOR.

THE DISCIPLES GREW INDIGNANT, NOT OUT OF SHOCK AT JAMES AND JOHN'S REQUEST, BUT BECAUSE THEY SECRETLY COVETED THE SAME THING FOR THEMSELVES.

(SEE LUKE 24:22.)

IF EVEN JESUS CAME TO EARTH TO SERVE, YOU ARE HERE TO SERVE, TOO.

BUT IN YOUR ZEAL TO SERVE, BE CAREFUL NOT TO WASTE YOUR TIME DOING OTHERS' WORK FOR THEM. YOU ARE STILL RESPONSIBLE FOR CASTING THE VISION.

MATTHEW 20:20-22, 24-28

Then the mother of Zebedee's sons came to Jesus with her sons and, kneeling down, asked a favor of him.

"What is it you want?" he asked. She said, "Grant that one of these two sons of mine may sit at your right and the other at your left in your kingdom."

"You don't know what you are asking," Jesus said to them. "Can you drink the cup I am going to drink?" "We can," they answered. . . .

When the ten heard about this, they were indignant with the two brothers.

Jesus called them together and said, "You know that the rulers of the Gentiles lord it over them, and their high officials exercise authority over them.

"Not so with you. Instead, whoever wants to become great among you must be your servant, and whoever wants to be first must be your slave—just as the Son of Man did not come to be served, but to serve, and to give his life as a ransom for many."

Four words in this passage are among the most powerful, meaningful, and significant in all the Bible: "Not so with you." With those four words Jesus sweeps away the entire power structure of the world and replaces it with a higher ethic. You want to be a leader? Great. Grab a towel and be a servant. Remember, Jesus came to serve others. Everything in his life flows from that simple fact. Everything in ours should flow from that same simple fact.

The "not so with you' statement says in a very simple but profound way that true followers of Christ are different. The standards and measurements of the world should not, must not, be the same for us. We must see the world and our role in it through a different set of lenses. Our interest in leadership cannot be about titles, power, prestige, and big offices. Our interest in leadership can only be about providing the leadership necessary to serve others in an optimum way.

Christian faith should change who we are. We must strive to see that the "not so with you" really differentiates us from those who are not yet followers of Jesus.

LEADERSHIP PRINCIPLE NUMBER 44

THE BEST LEADERS ARE THE BEST SERVANTS.

Is This Speaking to You?

Consider how well you're serving those who serve you. And consider some ways you can even the balance.

GOD'S WORD ON IT

Of all the great books out there on leadership styles and people skills, only one can claim to have all your answers.

THE WORD FOR THE DAY

WORLDLY WISDOM AND WAYS OF DOING THINGS CAN SOUND SO RIGHT SOMETIMES, BUT ONLY GOD'S WAY HAS THE RING OF TRUTH.

DON'T BE SPOOKED BY THE DISCIPLINE OF MEDITATION. DWELLING ON THE SCRIPTURE WILL CEMENT ITS TRUTHS IN YOUR LIFE.

STRIVE TO BE THE SAME IN BOTH "FRUIT" AND "LEAF"—IN BOTH THE PERSON YOU PROFESS TO BE AND THE PERSON YOU REALLY ARE.

THE BIBLE ISN'T TRUE BECAUSE IT WORKS. THE REASON IT WORKS IS BECAUSE IT'S TRUE.

PSALM 1:1-3
PSALM 19:7-11

Blessed is the man who does not walk in the counsel of the wicked or stand in the way of sinners or sit in the seat of mockers.

But his delight is in the law of the LORD, and on his law he meditates day and night.

He is like a tree planted by streams of water, which yields its fruit in season and whose leaf does not wither. Whatever he does prospers. . . .

The law of the LORD is perfect, reviving the soul. The statutes of the LORD are trustworthy, making wise the simple.

The precepts of the LORD are right, giving joy to the heart. The commands of the LORD are radiant, giving light to the eyes.

The fear of the LORD is pure, enduring forever. The ordinances of the LORD are sure and altogether righteous.

They are more precious than gold, than much pure gold; they are sweeter than honey, than honey from the comb.

By them is your servant warned; in keeping them there is great reward.

LEADERSHIP PRINCIPLE NUMBER 45

CHRISTIAN LEADERS MAKE A HABIT OF STUDYING THE BIBLE.

This may seem like I'm speaking to the wrong person. I mean, here you are reading a devotional book, already convinced that you need the Bible in order to make sense of your life. Let me assure you, as if you needed any more, that you have come to the right place to find your answers to life's questions.

But let me remind you, as well, that while the Bible is a very practical book, it is not limited to the practical. Too many times, we approach the Bible selfishly, concerned only with what it can say to us, how it can help us handle a specific issue that's on our plate. But God is much more than a cosmic answer man. He is God. And more than using His principles, He wants us to come to know Him, more each day. As we come to know Him, as He speaks to us through His Word, we learn about things much bigger than our everyday lives. We learn about who we really are. We learn about what really matters to Him. We learn about His plan for humanity and how we can pray and work more diligently through our leadership gifts to play our part in the drama.

Learn to love the Bible for all the right reasons.

Is This Speaking to You?

You can tell how seriously you're seeking the will of God by checking how much time you're seeking it in His Word.

SAY WHAT?

People listen to what you have to say. But sometimes the things you ***don't*** *say are the most eloquent words of all.*

THE WORD FOR THE DAY

JESUS WASN'T DODGING ANYTHING HERE. HE JUST WASN'T GIVING THEM THE SATISFACTION OF SEEING HIM CRACK.

WHEN YOU FEEL ANGER BURNING YOUR NECK, THAT'S WHEN YOU'LL KNOW WHETHER YOU HAVE YOUR TONGUE UNDER CONTROL.

JESUS WAS THE MASTER AT USING THE RIGHT WORDS. HE WASN'T AFRAID TO OFFEND, BUT ONLY TO MAKE PEOPLE SQUIRM AT THEIR OWN INDIFFERENCE.

"A GENTLE ANSWER TURNS AWAY WRATH, BUT A HARSH WORD STIRS UP ANGER" (PROVERBS 15:1).

MARK 14:53, 60-62A
MARK 15:1-5

They took Jesus to the high priest, and all the chief priests, elders and teachers of the law came together. . . .

Then the high priest stood up before them and asked Jesus, "Are you not going to answer? What is this testimony that these men are bringing against you?"

But Jesus remained silent and gave no answer. Again the high priest asked him, "Are you the Christ, the Son of the Blessed One?"

"I am," said Jesus. . . .

Very early in the morning, the chief priests, with the elders, the teachers of the law and the whole Sanhedrin, reached a decision. They bound Jesus, led him away and turned him over to Pilate.

"Are you the king of the Jews?" asked Pilate.

"Yes, it is as you say," Jesus replied.

The chief priests accused him of many things. So again Pilate asked him, "Aren't you going to answer? See how many things they are accusing you of."

But Jesus still made no reply, and Pilate was amazed.

LEADERSHIP PRINCIPLE NUMBER 46

LEADERS ARE CAREFUL ABOUT WHAT THEY SAY.

Unfortunately, God's name has become the expression of choice for many of my business associates. And what is even more distressing to me is that many men who consider themselves Christians have also begun using God's name in vain. I'm not sure why. You don't have to swear to make it or to be accepted in the business and professional worlds. I've known quite a few CEOs who did not even profess Christianity, yet never used profanity. It's more an issue of self-control and common decency. So if you've developed some bad habits in this area, clean it up. Pretend your kids are listening in on your conversations. Think about the image you're portraying and who you represent.

Do you know what you're going to do the next time an associate cuts loose with language that offends you? Make sure you've won the right to be heard. And when you discover your own language turning blue, get on your knees. God not only forgives, but gives you strength to throw out bad habits. Your language is often your calling card. Leave one behind that will reflect the purity and righteousness of Christ.

Is This Speaking to You?

Maybe you've already blown it in the last 24 hours. Maybe the next thing you need to say to someone is an apology.

IT'S FAMILY TIME

The best way to overcome the guilt of seeing your leadership role cost your family is to not make it cost them anymore.

THE WORD FOR THE DAY

YOUR CHILDREN WILL ONLY BE YOUNG ONCE. THINK TWICE BEFORE YOU TAKE EXTRA TIME AWAY FROM THEM.

WATCH FOR AS-YOU-GO OPPORTUNITIES TO TEACH SPIRITUAL LESSONS TO YOUR CHILDREN WITHIN THE FLOW OF LIFE.

SO YOU DON'T FORGET, KEEP A NOTEPAD WITH YOU TO JOT DOWN THINGS YOU WANT TO REMEMBER TO TELL YOUR KIDS.

TRY TO INVOLVE YOUR FAMILY AS MUCH AS POSSIBLE IN YOUR WORK.

GUARD AGAINST THE UNCHECKED WORDS OF WEARINESS AND FATIGUE.

DEUTERONOMY 6:5-9
PROVERBS 6:20-23

Hear, O Israel: The LORD our God, the LORD is one. Love the LORD your God with all your heart and with all your soul and with all your strength.

These commandments that I give you today are to be upon your hearts.

Impress them on your children. Talk about them when you sit at home and when you walk along the road, when you lie down and when you get up.

Tie them as symbols on your hands and bind them on your foreheads. Write them on the doorframes of your houses and on your gates. . . .

My son, keep your father's commands and do not forsake your mother's teaching. Bind them upon your heart for ever; fasten them around your neck.

When you walk, they will guide you; when you sleep, they will watch over you; when you awake, they will speak to you.

For these commands are a lamp, this teaching is a light, and the corrections of discipline are the way to life.

LEADERSHIP PRINCIPLE NUMBER 47

MAKE MORE THAN QUALITY TIME FOR YOUR FAMILY.

The wise and successful corporate leader will do all he can to take care of the children–his, those of his employees, and if his products are used by children, his customers.

Among the most important and productive things a corporate leader can do for the children of his employees is to do all he can to see that mothers and fathers spend time with their children. There is no way he can mandate quality time with the kids even if plenty of time off is allowed. However, a corporate executive can be sure that families and children are not shut out by the demands placed on parents. Managers can create a climate that honors and promotes balance.

There are lots of ways companies can let their employees know that their children are important to their employers. These range from big things such as company-sponsored college scholarships for the children of employees to small things such as recognizing the achievements of children in the corporate newsletter.

Remember what Jesus did. "He took the children in His arms, put His hands on them and blessed them" (Mark 10:16).

Is This Speaking to You?

Nothing wrong with being spontaneous, but what's something you can go ahead and plan to do together as a family?

ON LOAN FROM GOD

Your leadership gift doesn't make you better than anyone else. But it does make you responsible for investing it well.

THE WORD FOR THE DAY

PLAYING DOWN YOUR LEADERSHIP GIFT MAY HELP YOU FEEL HUMBLE, BUT IT TELLS GOD YOU'RE NOT HAPPY WITH WHAT HE GAVE YOU.

THE REASON GOD GAVE YOU YOUR SPECIFIC SKILLS IS "SO THAT THE BODY OF CHRIST MAY BE BUILT UP."

A CHURCH WHERE THE MEMBERS KNOW THEIR SPIRITUAL GIFTS AND ARE EXERCISING THEM CONSISTENTLY IS A CHURCH THAT IS OPERATING THE WAY GOD INTENDED.

EMBRACE YOUR CALLING AS YOUR "REASONABLE SERVICE" (ROMANS 12:1).

EPHESIANS 4:7, 11-16

But to each one of us grace has been given as Christ apportioned it. . . .

It was he who gave some to be apostles, some to be prophets, some to be evangelists, and some to be pastors and teachers, to prepare God's people for works of service, so that the body of Christ may be built up until we all reach unity in the faith and in the knowledge of the Son of God and become mature, attaining to the whole measure of the fullness of Christ.

Then we will no longer be infants, tossed back and forth by the waves, and blown here and there by every wind of teaching and by the cunning and craftiness of men in their deceitful scheming.

Instead, speaking the truth in love, we will in all things grow up into him who is the Head, that is, Christ.

From him the whole body, joined and held together by every supporting ligament, grows and builds itself up in love, as each part does its work.

LEADERSHIP PRINCIPLE NUMBER 48

LEADERSHIP IS A NOBLE SPIRITUAL GIFT TO BE HONORED AND HIGHLY ESTEEMED.

God has always called leaders and has uniquely gifted them to both lead his people and represent him in leadership areas among non-believers. Consider how many of the leaders in the Bible were leaders of the people of God and how many served in areas of leadership among unbelievers. Some, of course, did both.

Today, God still calls leaders to provide effective leadership for his people–his church–and he also calls them to represent him in leadership areas among those who do not serve him. If you think of the most influential areas of leadership in our society, you will note that the Gospel is terribly under-represented there. Our society pays a huge price for this. When Christians are not present to "salt" the thinking process, the forces of evil do it. We see this in the thinking projected by our media, our government, and our business community.

Christians must begin to take the gift of leadership much more seriously, and we must be willing to take the gift of God into the forums in our country where the tone of the nation is set. We need to lead effectively both inside and outside the church.

Is This Speaking to You?

Think bigger than your job description. Give God room to take you and your leadership skills anywhere He pleases.

OFF CENTER

If you try to do everything that everyone expects of you, you'll end up ***not*** *doing the things that are most important.*

THE WORD FOR THE DAY

JESUS KNEW THE PEOPLE WANTED . . . MORE! MORE! THAT IS ALWAYS THE CALL OF THE CROWD.

EVEN JESUS—WHO ACTUALLY DID CARRY THE WEIGHT OF THE WORLD ON HIS SHOULDERS—KNEW HOW TO SAY NO TO UNWISE DEMANDS.

WOULD YOU BE ABLE TO SPOT THE LINE IN YOUR OWN LIFE WHERE RESPONSIBILITY SLIPS OVER INTO EGO?

DELEGATE. THEY MAY NOT DO IT JUST THE WAY YOU WOULD. (NO, THEY MIGHT BE ABLE TO DO IT BETTER.)

LUKE 4:23-30

Jesus said to them, "Surely you will quote this proverb to me: 'Physician, heal yourself! Do here in your home town what we have heard that you did in Capernaum.' I tell you the truth," he continued, "no prophet is accepted in his home town.

"I assure you that there were many widows in Israel in Elijah's time, when the sky was shut for three and a half years and there was a severe famine throughout the land. Yet Elijah was not sent to any of them, but to a widow in Zarephath in the region of Sidon.

"And there were many in Israel with leprosy in the time of Elisha the prophet, yet not one of them was cleansed–only Naaman the Syrian."

All the people in the synagogue were furious when they heard this. They got up, drove him out of the town, and took him to the brow of the hill on which the town was built, in order to throw him down the cliff.

But he walked right through the crowd and went on his way.

LEADERSHIP PRINCIPLE NUMBER 49

LEADERS CANNOT LET THEIR SCHEDULE BE DETERMINED BY DISTRACTIONS.

One of a leader's first responsibilities is to establish order. We serve a God of order. A significant function of His act of creation was to bring order out of chaos.

Moving into any situation, an effective leader begins by creating order. Don't mistake a rigid, strict disciplinarian for a leader. That type of person does create order, but only for the sense of power and control it gives him. A leader creates order–in his own life as well as in the working environment of his employees–so he can more effectively serve others. For a leader, order is never merely an exercise of power, but a necessary part of preparation for service.

Contrary to popular opinion, order does not stifle creativity, but promotes it. It does not restrict freedom, but enhances it for the greatest number. Disorder is a kind of tyranny in which good things seldom happen. When disorder reigns, people suffer in many ways.

There is a difference between order and regimentation. Regimentation stifles creativity and restricts freedom, but order creates an environment where freedom and creativity–not distractions and chaos–can flourish.

Is This Speaking to You?

You'll be asked to do more than you can get done today. Decide ahead of time how you'll deal with distractions.

WATCHING YOUR BACK

Often as a leader, you have to trust your own judgment. But do you have someone to help you keep it trustworthy?

THE WORD FOR THE DAY

King Saul once received a similar rebuke, but responded with gasps and excuses instead of David's humble apologies.

The Lord met David and restored him. If God can give a second chance, shouldn't you?

David still paid dearly for his indiscretions. Don't think "I'm sorry" makes everything go away.

Return the favor. Offer yourself as an accountability partner to a friend or fellow Christian leader.

2 SAMUEL 12:1-4, 7, 9, 13

The LORD sent Nathan to David. When he came to him, he said, "There were two men in a certain town, one rich and the other poor. The rich man had a very large number of sheep and cattle, but the poor man had nothing except one little ewe lamb that he had bought.

"He raised it, and it grew up with him and his children. It shared his food, drank from his cup and even slept in his arms. It was like a daughter to him.

"Now a traveler came to the rich man, but the rich man refrained from taking one of his own sheep or cattle to prepare a meal for the traveler who had come to him. Instead, he took the ewe lamb that belonged to the poor man and prepared it for the one who had come to him. . . ."

Then Nathan said to David, "You are the man! . . . Why did you despise the word of the LORD by doing what is evil in his eyes? You did it in secret, but I will do this thing in broad daylight before all Israel." Then David said to Nathan, "I have sinned against the LORD."

LEADERSHIP PRINCIPLE NUMBER 50

WISE LEADERS MAKE THEMSELVES ACCOUNTABLE TO SOMEONE ELSE.

For many leaders, pride–a close relative of power–is the greatest of all leadership temptations. Looking good becomes more important than doing good. Leadership becomes the focus of the leader rather than the welfare of the organization and its people. And no leader is immune from the temptation.

Accountability is the best antidote for pride. Billy Graham understands this, and is always careful to keep a close circle of friends to whom he is accountable. He also credits his wife, Ruth, for help in this regard. I can relate to this. My own wife is quick to let me know when I begin to get "too big for my britches." Leaders need to be held accountable. A friend or group of friends who will tell you the truth and help keep pride in check is a must for sustaining godly leadership over time.

In the words of the old hymn, "Yield not to temptation, for yielding is sin; each victory will help you some other to win." No man can rise to leadership who has not experienced the truth of these words to some degree. Temptation comes with leadership. Understand this and prepare for it.

Is This Speaking to You?

How much better to heed a warning than to suffer the consequences. Have you activated your own security system?

TOTAL STEWARDSHIP

The way we talk about stewardship, you'd think money was all we cared about. But God cares about a lot more than that.

THE WORD FOR THE DAY

EVERYTHING WE HAVE BELONGS TO GOD. THAT ONE TRUTH SHOULD FOREVER CHANGE THE WAY WE VIEW THE THINGS AROUND US.

CHECK YOUR POLICY ON THIS: IS YOUR DOOR OPEN TO ANYONE WHO NEEDS WHAT YOU CAN GIVE?

IF YOU HAVE MANAGEMENT OVER OTHERS' RESOURCES, ALWAYS BE SURE YOU TREAT THEM AS IF THEY WERE YOUR OWN.

ALWAYS WANTING MORE CAN KEEP YOU ON AN ENDLESS CHASE, BUT GOOD STEWARDSHIP MAKES YOU CONTENT WITH WHAT YOU HAVE.

1 TIMOTHY 6:9-10, 17-19

People who want to get rich fall into temptation and a trap and into many foolish and harmful desires that plunge men into ruin and destruction.

For the love of money is a root of all kinds of evil. Some people, eager for money, have wandered from the faith and pierced themselves with many griefs.

But you, man of God, flee from all this, and pursue righteousness, godliness, faith, love, endurance and gentleness. . . .

Command those who are rich in this present world not to be arrogant nor to put their hope in wealth, which is so uncertain, but to put their hope in God, who richly provides us with everything for our enjoyment.

Command them to do good, to be rich in good deeds, and to be generous and willing to share.

In this way they will lay up treasure for themselves as a firm foundation for the coming age, so that they may take hold of the life that is truly life.

LEADERSHIP PRINCIPLE NUMBER 51

THE BEST LEADERS KNOW HOW TO BE GOOD STEWARDS OF ALL THEIR RESOURCES.

American Christians seem to be especially susceptible to the "more than enough" mindset, so in general, I recommend great caution when it comes to money. It is so easy to believe that God wants us to be the wealthiest people on earth, when all He really wants is our obedience.

Please understand that I'm not advocating a no-growth position or asking you to live like a hermit. I shudder to think what the Christian community would look like if we all eschewed the earning of money. As a businessman, I know the importance of growth, and I do my best to help my company earn more this year than they did last year. Excellence should always be our goal as Christians in business, for our work is one way in which we honor Christ.

But the ability to earn money and use it properly is what stewardship is all about. I fully subscribe to John Wesley's admonition to earn all you can and save all you can so that you may give all you can. We must, however, understand that the only "more" which will really satisfy us is having more of God in our lives. He, and He alone, can quench our thirst for more.

Is This Speaking to You?

You have a lot more than money in your pocket of blessings. Are you willing to turn them inside out for His glory?

OPPORTUNITY CALLS

The greatest victories you will win as a leader will be the ones that seemed the most unwinnable at the start.

THE WORD FOR THE DAY

"BE STRONG AND COURAGEOUS." THERE IS NO SUBSTITUTE FOR BOLDNESS AND NO VICTORY WITHOUT A FIGHT.

MOSES' DEATH LEFT JOSHUA WITH SOME BIG SHOES TO FILL. DO YOU SOMETIMES FEEL LIKE YOU'RE IN OVER YOUR HEAD? RELAX. YOU'RE IN GOOD COMPANY.

GOD TOLD JOSHUA TO REFER TO HIS WORD FOR GUIDANCE. THE BIBLE IS FULL OF PROMISES. READ THEM. BELIEVE THEM.

MAKE THOUGHTFUL PLANS TO MOVE AHEAD WITH YOUR ESTABLISHED OBJECTIVES, THEN PROCEED WITH PRAYER AND ACTION.

JOSHUA 1:6-11A, 16

"Be strong and courageous, because you will lead these people to inherit the land I swore to their forefathers to give them.

"Be strong and very courageous. Be careful to obey all the law my servant Moses gave you; do not turn from it to the right or to the left, that you may be successful wherever you go.

"Do not let this Book of the Law depart from your mouth; meditate on it day and night, so that you may be careful to do everything written in it. Then you will be prosperous and successful.

"Have I not commanded you? Be strong and courageous. Do not be terrified; do not be discouraged, for the LORD your God will be with you wherever you go."

So Joshua ordered the officers of the people: "Go through the camp and tell the people, 'Get your supplies ready. Three days from now you will cross the Jordan. . . .' "

Then they answered Joshua, "Whatever you have commanded us we will do, and wherever you send us we will go.

LEADERSHIP PRINCIPLE NUMBER 52

LEADERS SEE CHALLENGES AS OPPORTUNITIES.

Leaders lead, managers manage. A pure manager, when faced with a situation outside the system, is unsure of how to respond. A pure leader, on the other hand, revels in the unexpected and responds with innovative brilliance.

No other leader will have the supernatural ability of Jesus to know what those around him are thinking. But a leader must have the ability to evaluate a situation on the spot, get a feel for what is taking place, and make the situation work for good.

My longtime friend and business partner, Donald Dell, is one of the all-time great negotiators, negotiating some of the most famous contracts in professional sports. Much of this talent stems from his ability to discern what others are thinking and feeling. In a room filled with lawyers, accountants, and managers–often hostile and adversarial–Donald has the uncanny ability to sense their mood and tailor his responses accordingly.

A leader is ready to respond in positive ways to the unexpected, consistently analyzing situations and responding with boldness as he is led by the Holy Spirit.

Is This Speaking to You?

Try not to concentrate so much on the obstacles that lie ahead as on the reward that's waiting just beyond them.

OUT IN THE OPEN

Some people seem to look for conflict, others to avoid it. Smart leaders know when to let it go and when to air it out.

THE WORD FOR THE DAY

PAUL OPPOSED PETER "TO HIS FACE." THAT'S ALWAYS BETTER THAN OPPOSING SOMEONE BEHIND THEIR BACK.

PETER HAD THE INFLUENCE TO SET POLICY AND PRECEDENT IN THE EARLY CHURCH. AND PAUL HAD THE COURAGE TO FORCE HIM TO RECONSIDER HIS POSITION.

"EVEN BARNABAS WAS LED ASTRAY." IF IMPORTANT ISSUES ARE LEFT UNRESOLVED, GOOD PEOPLE GET HURT BAD.

LEADERS CAN'T LET EVEN THE FAMILIAR TUG OF FRIENDSHIP KEEP THEM FROM POINTING OUT GLARING ERRORS.

GALATIANS 2:11-14, 19-20

When Peter came to Antioch, I opposed him to his face, because he was clearly in the wrong.

Before certain men came from James, he used to eat with the Gentiles. But when they arrived, he began to draw back and separate himself from the Gentiles because he was afraid of those who belonged to the circumcision group.

The other Jews joined him in his hypocrisy, so that by their hypocrisy even Barnabas was led astray.

When I saw that they were not acting in line with the truth of the gospel, I said to Peter in front of them all, "You are a Jew, yet you live like a Gentile and not like a Jew. How is it, then, that you force Gentiles to follow Jewish customs? . . .

For through the law I died to the law so that I might live for God.

I have been crucified with Christ and I no longer live, but Christ lives in me. The life I live in the body, I live by faith in the Son of God, who loved me and gave himself for me.

LEADERSHIP PRINCIPLE NUMBER 53

TIMES OF CRISIS OVER FUNDAMENTAL VALUES MUST BE FACED SQUARELY AND HONESTLY.

So much time and productivity are lost because disputes are allowed to drag on unsettled. A good leader will have and enforce a policy that calls for immediate face-to-face resolution of disputes. To allow them to linger, grow, and fester is always counterproductive. Advantage is almost never gained through delay.

For some reason Christians have a particularly difficult time confronting each other in love, settling whatever the dispute might be, and then moving on in friendship and respect, regardless of the way the question is settled. All too often, the issue is never squarely faced, leading to disunity and uneasy relationships. Or if it is faced, one party all too often leaves if the decision is considered adverse. Both approaches are definitely unscriptural. Jesus said, "Settle matters quickly with your adversary." (Matthew 5:25).

Disputes and disagreements will occur, but leaders need to be ready for them. Everyone involved should be heard. A decision should be reached and communicated. Then all parties should move on to the next challenge.

Is This Speaking to You?

The first step toward defending the things you care about is to care about things that are worth defending.

SHARING THE LOAD

Every time you hand off some task or assignment, you're making an investment in someone else, as well as in yourself.

THE WORD FOR THE DAY

YOU THINK *YOUR* JOB IS TOUGH. MOSES HAD ASSUMED TOTAL RESPONSIBILITY FOR JUDGING THE DISPUTES OF MORE THAN 3 MILLION PEOPLE.

JETHRO REPRIMANDED MOSES FOR HIS POOR MANAGEMENT. ALWAYS BE WILLING TO ACCEPT SOUND ADVICE—EVEN FROM YOUR IN-LAWS!

MOSES WAS TOLD TO "SELECT CAPABLE MEN." NOT JUST ANYONE WILL DO WHEN YOU DELEGATE.

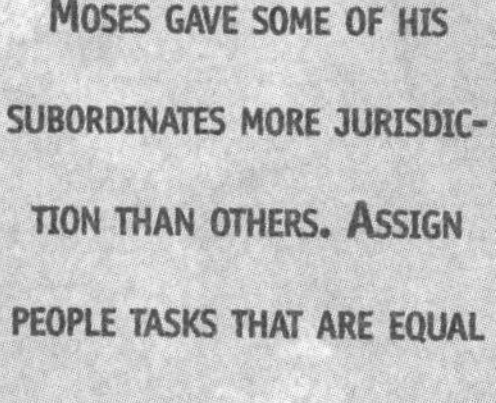

MOSES GAVE SOME OF HIS SUBORDINATES MORE JURISDICTION THAN OTHERS. ASSIGN PEOPLE TASKS THAT ARE EQUAL TO THEIR CAPABILITIES.

EXODUS 18:14-15, 17-19, 21-22

When his father-in-law saw all that Moses was doing for the people, he said, "What is this you are doing for the people? Why do you alone sit as judge, while all these people stand round you from morning till evening?"

Moses answered him, "Because the people come to me to seek God's will. . . ."

Moses' father-in-law replied, . . . "Listen now to me and I will give you some advice, and may God be with you. You must be the people's representative before God and bring their disputes to him. . . .

"But select capable men from all the people–men who fear God, trustworthy men who hate dishonest gain–and appoint them as officials over thousands, hundreds, fifties and tens.

"Have them serve as judges for the people at all times, but have them bring every difficult case to you; the simple cases they can decide themselves. That will make your load lighter, because they will share it with you."

Authority is the very essence of leadership. How it is established, exercised, and particularly how it is delegated will determine to a great extent your effectiveness as a leader.

Be sure you know the extent of your authority. Exercise all of it, but no more. Leaders are less than they should be when they refuse to exercise the authority they have, or when they attempt to exceed the authority they have been granted.

Proper delegation of authority as delivered in this passage is of great importance. Quality delegation extends the reach of your leadership. It allows you to concentrate on those tasks which only you can accomplish. It keeps you from getting bogged down in details better handled by someone else. Most importantly, it helps you train future leaders, including your own replacement, a requirement for all successful leaders.

Wise leaders understand that any authority granted to them ultimately comes from God. Jesus said, "All authority in heaven and on earth has been given to me" (Matthew 28:18). A wise leader exercises his authority, understanding that he is acting as an agent of the Lord.

LEADERSHIP PRINCIPLE NUMBER 54

WISE LEADERS DO NOT TRY TO DO IT ALL BY THEMSELVES.

Is This Speaking to You?

What are the top three items on your to-do list that never get done? Could someone else do what you can't get to?

HONESTLY

You're not a bald-faced liar. But has it become easy to tell less than you know, to cloak the truth in prettier clothes?

THE WORD FOR THE DAY

YOU'LL BE GLAD YOU WERE UP-FRONT WITH PEOPLE TODAY INSTEAD OF HAVING TO COVER YOUR OWN TRACKS TOMORROW.

HONESTY IS ABOUT MUCH MORE THAN YOUR WORDS. HONESTY IS A WAY OF LIFE, A LOOK ON YOUR FACE, A PURITY IN ALL YOUR MOTIVES.

THERE IS NO SUBSTITUTE FOR "A CLEAR CONSCIENCE." YOU CAN WITHSTAND A LOT OF HEAT WHEN YOUR OWN HEART CAN DEFEND YOU.

"LIVE PEACEFUL AND QUIET LIVES IN ALL GODLINESS AND HOLINESS" (1 TIMOTHY 2:2).

HEBREWS 13:15-21

Through Jesus, therefore, let us continually offer to God a sacrifice of praise–the fruit of lips that confess his name. And do not forget to do good and to share with others, for with such sacrifices God is pleased.

Obey your leaders and submit to their authority. They keep watch over you as men who must give an account. Obey them so that their work will be a joy, not a burden, for that would be of no advantage to you.

Pray for us. We are sure that we have a clear conscience and desire to live honorably in every way. I particularly urge you to pray so that I may be restored to you soon.

May the God of peace, who through the blood of the eternal covenant brought back from the dead our Lord Jesus, that great Shepherd of the sheep, equip you with everything good for doing his will, and may he work in us what is pleasing to him, through Jesus Christ, to whom be glory for ever and ever. Amen.

LEADERSHIP PRINCIPLE NUMBER 55

ALWAYS BE HONEST.

The ninth commandment tells us not to lie. You may think you are a very truthful person, but every time you do not do what you say you will do, you tell a lie. Particularly in business, we have become cavalier about not doing what we say we will do. "I'll call you tomorrow." "We'll get together soon for lunch." "I'll shoot you a fax on that ASAP." "I will be there by 10 a.m. sharp." "You'll have a signed contract on your desk by noon Monday." Too often, we make these kinds of statements without a real commitment to being sure we do our part in making them happen.

Unfortunately, Christians in business can be as bad about not making promised phone calls, not delivering as promised, not being punctual–not doing what we say we will do–as non-Christians. While there may be some circumstances beyond our control that prevent us from doing what we say we will do, these should be rare exceptions, not the rule. And when they do occur, we should be very quick to apologize and make it very clear that we are disappointed that our performance has not measured up to our promise.

Is This Speaking to You?

Make up your mind that you will always face every question honestly, every problem squarely, every person openly.

ONE DAY, ONE STEP

God's timeframe can seem very slow to this world's way of thinking. But who do you think knows the best way?

THE WORD FOR THE DAY

ABRAHAM AND SARAH GOT IMPATIENT AND SOUGHT A MORE LOGICAL WAY TO GOD'S WILL. TRUST HIM TO MAKE GOOD ON HIS PROMISES, BUT IN HIS OWN TIME.

THEIR PLAN SEEMED FOOLPROOF, BUT RESULTED IN ANGER, DISCORD, AND PERMANENT DAMAGE TO THEIR FAMILY.

ACTIONS HAVE CONSEQUENCES, NOT ONLY FOR THE SHORT RUN, BUT EVEN MORE DRAMATICALLY FOR THE LONG TERM.

SHORT CUTS WILL RARELY TAKE YOU TO YOUR DESIRED DESTINATION, AND NEVER IN THE WAY GOD INTENDED.

GENESIS 16:1-6

Now Sarai, Abram's wife, had borne him no children. But she had an Egyptian maidservant named Hagar; so she said to Abram, "The LORD has kept me from having children. Go, sleep with my maidservant; perhaps I can build a family through her." Abram agreed to what Sarai said.

So after Abram had been living in Canaan ten years, Sarai his wife took her Egyptian maidservant Hagar and gave her to her husband to be his wife.

He slept with Hagar, and she conceived. When she knew she was pregnant, she began to despise her mistress.

Then Sarai said to Abram, "You are responsible for the wrong I am suffering. I put my servant in your arms, and now that she knows she is pregnant, she despises me. May the LORD judge between you and me."

"Your servant is in your hands," Abram said. "Do with her whatever you think best." Then Sarai ill-treated Hagar; so she fled from her.

LEADERSHIP PRINCIPLE NUMBER 56

THE END NEVER JUSTIFIES THE MEANS. WE MUST TRY TO ADHERE TO GOD'S TIMING.

Shortcuts are always seductive. It is always tempting to look for an easier way to get something done. But the quick, easy, and cheap almost never work. In the long run they turn out to be slow, hard, and expensive.

Leaders need to understand the difference between the tempting shortcut and the most efficient way to accomplish something. There is a vast difference. Most things of quality are built slowly over time and come at a significant price. Some think that building a church or a business is best accomplished by grandstand plays, a form of a shortcut. They look for big flashy promotions, huge and inflated publicity. These do make a splash, but the ripples soon disappear and nothing remains. Those enterprises built on hard work, one quality step at a time, are the ones that endure.

There are no shortcuts to becoming a mature Christian. Time spent in God's Word, prayer, and faith-building acts of obedience, *over time*, is the only formula. There are no quick fixes.

God's timing is always best. Enduring faith in God's promises is the way to success.

Is This Speaking to You?

Is God's plan taking longer to develop than you thought? Wait him out anyway. You'll never think of a better one.

OPEN TO ANYTHING

The world in which you lead can be all-consuming at times, but serving in God's Kingdom is all-important all the time.

THE WORD FOR THE DAY

PAUL WANTED TO TAKE THE GOSPEL NORTH, BUT WHEN THE SPIRIT LED HIM WEST, HE FOLLOWED WILLINGLY.

IT DOESN'T SAY HOW THE SPIRIT PREVENTED THEM. BUT IT'S CLEAR THAT GOD HAS WAYS OF MAKING HIS DIRECTION KNOWN.

DECISIONS THAT ARE SEEMINGLY SMALL CAN HAVE AN ENORMOUS IMPACT ON THE FUTURE.

PAUL WAS JOINED IN HIS EFFORTS BY A NUMBER OF COMPANIONS. DO YOU HAVE FRIENDS ALONGSIDE TO HELP YOU RECOGNIZE GOD'S COURSE OF ACTION?

ACTS 16:6-10, 13-14

Paul and his companions traveled throughout the region of Phrygia and Galatia, having been kept by the Holy Spirit from preaching the word in the province of Asia.

When they came to the border of Mysia, they tried to enter Bithynia, but the Spirit of Jesus would not allow them to. So they passed by Mysia and went down to Troas.

During the night Paul had a vision of a man of Macedonia standing and begging him, "Come over to Macedonia and help us." After Paul had seen the vision, we got ready at once to leave for Macedonia, concluding that God had called us to preach the gospel to them. . . .

On the Sabbath we went outside the city gate to the river, where we expected to find a place of prayer. We sat down and began to speak to the women who had gathered there.

One of those listening was a woman named Lydia, a dealer in purple cloth from the city of Thyatira, who was a worshiper of God. The Lord opened her heart to respond to Paul's message.

LEADERSHIP PRINCIPLE NUMBER 57

STAY FOCUSED ON YOUR MISSION, BUT FLEXIBLE TO YOUR CIRCUMSTANCES AND TO GOD'S SPIRIT.

This short passage may not seem to be important, but it contains many very instructive leadership lessons. It shows both the importance of a team as well as the importance of a leader. It particularly points out the necessity of a godly leader, one who is in touch with and sensitive to the direction of the Holy Spirit.

Among the most important leadership lessons this passage teaches is perseverance. When we are sure what the goal is, when we know that our mission has worth, we should not be discouraged by obstacles and temporary failure. Keep at it. Find another way. Find another place. Find a way to accomplish the mission. Be ready to move on to more productive areas.

Yet while perseverance is tremendously important, flexibility is also vital. Some leaders are so determined to get it done their way, to get it done in a place of their choosing, they waste tremendous energy and great resources. Do as Paul and his team did. If after a good solid effort you fail in one place or with one technique, don't abandon the mission, but move to another place or adopt another approach.

Is This Speaking to You?

Are your plans for the day flexible enough to be changed if you sense God taking you down another road?

CAREFUL CUTBACKS

Trimming your staff is one of the hardest things you'll ever have to do as a leader. And strangely, one of the best.

THE WORD FOR THE DAY

THOSE IN GIDEON'S ARMY WHO WERE AFRAID OR NOT READY FOR THE CHALLENGE WOULD HAVE HELD BACK THE EFFORT. PERSONAL ISSUES CAN OFTEN THREATEN THE GREATER GOOD.

FEW THINGS DISRUPT A PERSON'S LIFE LIKE BEING ELIMINATED FROM THEIR JOB. BE VERY SURE YOU HAVE TRIED ALL OTHER OPTIONS FIRST.

CUTTING SOMEONE LOOSE CAN OFTEN BE THE BEST THING FOR EVERYONE. ALMOST INVARIABLY, GOD LEADS SOMEONE TO A BETTER PLACE, A BETTER FIT, ONE THEY WOULD NEVER HAVE CHOSEN ON THEIR OWN.

JUDGES 7:2-4A, 5-7

The LORD said to Gideon, "You have too many men for me to deliver Midian into their hands. In order that Israel may not boast against me that her own strength has saved her, announce now to the people, 'Anyone who trembles with fear may turn back and leave Mount Gilead.'" So twenty-two thousand men left, while ten thousand remained.

But the LORD said to Gideon, "There are still too many men. Take them down to the water, and I will sift them out for you there. . . .

So Gideon took the men down to the water. There the LORD told him, "Separate those who lap the water with their tongues like a dog from those who kneel down to drink."

Three hundred men lapped with their hands to their mouths. All the rest got down on their knees to drink.

The LORD said to Gideon, "With the three hundred men that lapped I will save you and give the Midianites into your hands. Let all the other men go, each to his own place."

BRINER NOTES

LEADERSHIP PRINCIPLE NUMBER 58

A SMALL FORCE CAN OFTEN BE MORE EFFECTIVE THAN A LARGER ONE. PRUNE FOR PRODUCTIVITY.

Unity is a leadership essential. A wise leader will sacrifice much to produce a unified group of people. A smaller unified group is always more productive than a larger divided one.

Sports provides a good way to see this principle with clarity. Smart coaches will always sacrifice talent and numbers for unity. That's why you'll often see very talented players traded or released. A coach would rather have a smaller squad in which everyone has a definite role to play, than a larger one where players are being disruptive and becoming sources of disunity. Jesus teaches us to prune for productivity.

The same principle certainly applies to business. Downsizing of American businesses has been roundly criticized in many quarters. Yet it has helped produce the most vibrant economy–as well as the lowest unemployment–the nation has ever known. Biblical principles, once again, work in the marketplace. People are never to be seen as pawns in a grand scheme, and downsizing should never be done cavalierly or inhumanely, but sometimes it must be done for the overall good of everyone.

Is This Speaking to You?

If personnel problems are continuing to sidetrack you, ask God to show you the wisest way to handle them.

MONEY MATTERS

Money is neither good nor bad. But leaders who learn how to manage it wisely can make it work like God intended.

THE WORD FOR THE DAY

EFFECTIVE MONEY MANAGEMENT AND HARD WORK ARE COMPANION VIRTUES.

GOD IS THE TRUE GIVER OF IT ALL, BUT HE ENTRUSTS US TO PROVIDE FOR OURSELVES AND OUR FAMILIES.

HANDLING MONEY WISELY SETS A GOOD EXAMPLE FOR OTHERS.

SELF-DISCIPLINE IS THE FIRST PREREQUISITE FOR FAITHFUL STEWARDSHIP.

WHENEVER YOU'RE MANAGING OTHERS' MONEY OR DONATIONS, ALWAYS TREAT IT WITH THE SAME CARE AS IF IT WERE YOUR OWN.

2 THESSALONIANS 3:6-13

In the name of the Lord Jesus Christ, we command you, brothers, to keep away from every brother who is idle and does not live according to the teaching you received from us.

For you yourselves know how you ought to follow our example. We were not idle when we were with you, nor did we eat anyone's food without paying for it. On the contrary, we worked night and day, laboring and toiling so that we would not be a burden to any of you.

We did this, not because we do not have the right to such help, but in order to make ourselves a model for you to follow.

For even when we were with you, we gave you this rule: "If a man will not work, he shall not eat."

We hear that some among you are idle. They are not busy; they are busybodies. Such people we command and urge in the Lord Jesus Christ to settle down and earn the bread they eat.

And as for you, brothers, never tire of doing what is right.

LEADERSHIP PRINCIPLE NUMBER 59

MANAGE YOUR MONEY WITH WISDOM AND INTEGRITY.

You can make a lot of money and not know how to manage money. Many companies bring in millions on the topline, but have little to show for it on the bottom line. There are many reasons for this, but certainly the ability of leaders to manage money wisely–and to motivate their employees to the same kind of discipline–has a lot to do with this scenario.

I think it is best to view money for what it is–a means to an end. Money is not an objective, but rather a strategic part of achieving your objectives. It is not a goal, but is an ingredient in helping you meet your goals. Whenever a dollar figure becomes a sole aim, you can be sure you've lost the proper perspective of money in your organization.

Money is not something to apologize for. I'm not saying that it is unnecessary. Indeed, it is vital in order for your enterprise to succeed. But money is merely a tool that allows you to provide a better service, or produce a better product, or reach a larger number of people.

Making sure that you have enough money is no problem to God. But can He trust you to manage it?

Is This Speaking to You?

Whether in the financial worlds of family budgets or company spreadsheets, ask God to help you handle money well.

DAY SIXTY

READY FOR ANYTHING

Leaders know that getting themselves ready to start the day involves a lot more than deodorant and a doughnut.

THE WORD FOR THE DAY

PLANNING AHEAD WILL MAKE YOUR DRIVETIME A LOT MORE PEACEFUL, YOUR INNER CONVERSATIONS MORE LIKE PRAYERS AND LESS LIKE REHEARSALS.

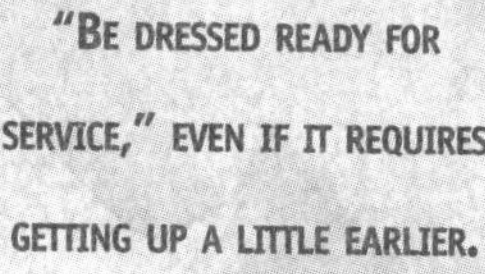

"BE DRESSED READY FOR SERVICE," EVEN IF IT REQUIRES GETTING UP A LITTLE EARLIER.

HAVE YOU FIGURED SOME TIME FOR MINISTRY INTO YOUR DAY? AND ARE YOU WILLING TO ADJUST YOUR SCHEDULE IF GOD TAKES YOU IN ANOTHER DIRECTION?

IT'S FAIR TO ASK GOD TO MULTIPLY YOUR TIME AND EFFORTS WHEN UNAVOIDABLE DELAYS HAVE PUT YOU BEHIND.

LUKE 12:35-38, 42-44

"Be dressed ready for service and keep your lamps burning, like men waiting for their master to return from a wedding banquet, so that when he comes and knocks they can immediately open the door for him.

It will be good for those servants whose master finds them watching when he comes. I tell you the truth, he will dress himself to serve, will have them recline at the table and will come and wait on them.

It will be good for those servants whose master finds them ready, even if he comes in the second or third watch of the night. . . .

The Lord answered, "Who then is the faithful and wise manager, whom the master puts in charge of his servants to give them their food allowance at the proper time?

It will be good for that servant whom the master finds doing so when he returns. I tell you the truth, he will put him in charge of all his possessions.

LEADERSHIP PRINCIPLE NUMBER 60

LEADERS DO THEIR HOMEWORK. THEY ENTER INTO EACH DAY PREPARED.

In my forty years in business, I have rarely felt overprepared. I have often felt severely underprepared, and the results have borne out that feeling. Inadequate preparation produces inadequate results.

Jesus powerfully taught us about preparation, both by His own perfect example and by His teaching. Many of the parables He used to explain His principles admonish us to be well prepared. For example, the parable of the foolish virgins, who were caught without oil in their lamps when the bridegroom came and thus missed the wedding, teaches us about adequate preparation. So also does the parable of the servants, who did not perform their assigned tasks and were not ready to meet their master upon His return. They thought the master would be away a long time, so they wasted their time and received the master's wrath when he returned unexpectedly.

Whether you're laying the foundation for a career, launching a product, or making a presentation, there is no substitute for preparation. Give it the necessary time and attention. Jesus did. His amazing success is a testimony to its importance.

Is This Speaking to You?

If you're always going too fast to take time to gather your thoughts, maybe you're going too fast to begin with.

EXPERIENCE TELLS ME

Good leaders never stop learning. But the best ones try to avoid having to learn the same lessons over and over again.

THE WORD FOR THE DAY

ARROGANCE CAN PUMP YOU FULL OF UNWISE, UNCHALLENGED CONCLUSIONS. HUMILITY WILL MAKE YOU LESS LIABLE TO COURT DISASTER.

"MY EARS HAD HEARD OF YOU BUT NOW MY EYES HAVE SEEN YOU." THERE'S NO SUBSTITUTE FOR SEEING WHAT GOD CAN DO FIRSTHAND.

THERE IS A SPIRITUAL REWARD TO BEING MEEK BEFORE GOD, BUT A VERY NATURAL REWARD FOR THOSE WHO LEARN FROM THEIR MISTAKES.

MAKE IT YOUR DESIRE TO DIE "OLD AND FULL OF YEARS," NOT JUST IN AGE, BUT IN WISDOM.

JOB 42:1-6, 12-13, 16-17

Then Job replied to the LORD: "I know that you can do all things; no plan of yours can be thwarted.

"You asked, 'Who is this that obscures my counsel without knowledge?' Surely I spoke of things I did not understand, things too wonderful for me to know.

"You said, 'Listen now, and I will speak; I will question you, and you shall answer me.'

"My ears had heard of you but now my eyes have seen you. Therefore I despise myself and repent in dust and ashes . . ."

The LORD blessed the latter part of Job's life more than the first. He had fourteen thousand sheep, six thousand camels, a thousand yoke of oxen and a thousand donkeys. And he also had seven sons and three daughters. . . .

After this, Job lived a hundred and forty years; he saw his children and their children to the fourth generation.

And so he died, old and full of years.

LEADERSHIP PRINCIPLE NUMBER 61

WISE LEADERS ARE ABLE TO BUILD ON PAST EXPERIENCE.

Management gurus from Warren Buffet to Tom Peters have noted the importance of corporate culture to the success of an enterprise. Corporate culture is built primarily on the stories of both corporate success and corporate failure. Those stories need to be told and retold, and their truths need to be applied to situations currently facing a company.

Jesus did this in two ways. He told Old Testament stories, using the Scriptures to great effect, and He used parables to communicate some of the most important lessons He needed to share.

Frito-Lay, the giant snack-food arm of Pepsico, has a legendary distribution system. Many writers have attested to it by repeating stories of the lengths to which Frito-Lay's delivery men have gone to get even the smallest order to the most remote customer. Other companies have their own stories upon which their corporate culture is based. Successful managers tell these war stories over and over as a way of teaching how things should be done–or not done.

Make sure you know the legends, lore, and parables of your company. Use them to inspire.

Is This Speaking to You?

Keeping a journal you can refer to from a distance is one of the best ways to learn from the past, prepare for the future.

GOALTENDING

Setting goals can eat into your work time. But trying to work without them will eat away your effectiveness.

THE WORD FOR THE DAY

WE MEASURE OUR LIVES IN YEARS, BUT GOD MEASURES THEM IN DAYS—THE SINGLE STEPS WE TAKE ON THE WAY TO OUR FUTURE.

BE SURE TO ATTACH ACTIONS TO YOUR GOALS SO YOU DON'T REMAIN FOREVER STUCK IN THE PLANNING STAGE.

YOU'LL NEED OTHERS TO HELP YOU ACHIEVE YOUR GOALS. DON'T TRY TO DO IT ALL YOURSELF. SHARE THE DREAM, THE LOAD, AND THE REWARD.

KEEP THE END GOAL IN SIGHT AT ALL TIMES. THEN YOU'LL KNOW WHEN YOU GET THERE.

1 KINGS 6:1-2, 11-13, 37-38

In the four hundred and eightieth year after the Israelites had come out of Egypt, in the fourth year of Solomon's reign over Israel, in the month of Ziv, the second month, he began to build the temple of the LORD.

The temple that King Solomon built for the LORD was sixty cubits long, twenty wide and thirty high. . . .

The word of the LORD came to Solomon: "As for this temple you are building, if you follow my decrees, carry out my regulations and keep all my commands and obey them, I will fulfill through you the promise I gave to David your father. And I will live among the Israelites and will not abandon my people Israel. . . ."

The foundation of the temple of the LORD was laid in the fourth year, in the month of Ziv.

In the eleventh year in the month of Bul, the eighth month, the temple was finished in all its details according to its specifications. He had spent seven years building it.

LEADERSHIP PRINCIPLE NUMBER 62

SET AMBITIOUS GOALS AND MONITOR YOUR PROGRESS REGULARLY.

Jesus spoke of a narrow way, a path that runs counter to the prevailing winds of public opinion and routine expectations. A way that requires firm resolve and a set pattern of following lifelong goals. Almost all business success to some degree is based on this instruction. Every great business has in some way found a narrow way, a way that others were not able or not willing to go, a way that required a vision, followed by a step-by-step plan on how to get there. This is what sets a company apart and makes it special and successful.

The narrow way should always be our goal, in every aspect of life. Those managers hoping for success should look for ways to set themselves apart in positive ways from those who walk blithely down the broad path with no destination in sight.

Spending more hours on the job is not necessarily the way to do this. Try caring more about quality than others do. Try serving your customers and those who work for you better than anyone else. Try to have the most congenial work environment in your company. These are narrow ways that lead to success.

Is This Speaking to You?

What is God asking of you? Put it into words, then put it to a plan—then watch Him help you put it into action.

PURE MOTIVATION

Every leader has people who are aggravating and hard to motivate. But when you lead with love, good things follow.

THE WORD FOR THE DAY

JESUS HAD EVERY REASON TO SEE NOTHING BUT THE BAD IN HIS RAG-TAG GROUP OF FOLLOWERS, BUT HE CHOSE TO LOVE THEM INSTEAD.

FRIENDS. IS THAT HOW YOU FEEL ABOUT THOSE WHO ANSWER TO YOU?

HELPING PEOPLE "BEAR FRUIT—FRUIT THAT WILL LAST" SHOULD BE THE PRIMARY GOAL OF YOUR MOTIVATIONAL STRATEGIES. PRODUCTIVE INDIVIDUALS RESULT IN A PRODUCTIVE WHOLE.

GENUINE LOVE FOR OTHERS HAS A WAY OF BEING CONTAGIOUS. IF YOU START THE PROCESS, PEOPLE WILL FOLLOW.

JOHN 15:9-17

"As the Father has loved me, so have I loved you. Now remain in my love. If you obey my commands, you will remain in my love, just as I have obeyed my Father's commands and remain in his love.

"I have told you this so that my joy may be in you and that your joy may be complete. My command is this: Love each other as I have loved you.

"Greater love has no one than this, that he lay down his life for his friends. You are my friends if you do what I command.

"I no longer call you servants, because a servant does not know his master's business. Instead, I have called you friends, for everything that I learned from my Father I have made known to you.

"You did not choose me, but I chose you and appointed you to go and bear fruit–fruit that will last. Then the Father will give you whatever you ask in my name. This is my command: Love each other."

LEADERSHIP PRINCIPLE NUMBER 63

TRUE LEADERS MOTIVATE WITHOUT MANIPULATING.

Jesus, the greatest of all leaders, clearly represents the special relationship that can evolve between leaders and followers. He never exhibited a cool detachment toward His followers. They were not simply pawns to carry out His wishes and implement His plans. His followers were very special to Him and, conversely, He was very special to them. This mutually caring, mutually productive, mutually protective, non-exploitive leader/follower relationship that Jesus maintained with His disciples is a model for all leaders to follow.

The idea that leaders should treat all followers exactly the same is a myth. Trying to do this actually inhibits the kind of intimacy necessary for the most positive type of leadership to emerge. In order to lead a large number effectively, it is always necessary to have a deeper, more personal, more intense relationship with those who follow you.

Good leaders have a vision. Better leaders share a vision. The best leaders invite others to join them in spreading the vision. Shared vision binds leaders and followers together in a way that little else can.

Is This Speaking to You?

Ask God to help you love those under your leadership, even the ones who cause you the most trouble.

DAY SIXTY-FOUR

WHAT DO *YOU* THINK?

People look to you for making good decisions and handling tough issues. Do you look to anyone to help you do it well?

THE WORD FOR THE DAY

1 KINGS 12:1-7

Rehoboam went to Shechem, for all the Israelites had gone there to make him king.

When Jeroboam son of Nebat heard this (he was still in Egypt, where he had fled from King Solomon), he returned from Egypt.

So they sent for Jeroboam, and he and the whole assembly of Israel went to Rehoboam and said to him: "Your father put a heavy yoke on us, but now lighten the harsh labor and the heavy yoke he put on us, and we will serve you."

Rehoboam answered, "Go away for three days and then come back to me." So the people went away.

Then King Rehoboam consulted the elders who had served his father Solomon during his lifetime. "How would you advise me to answer these people?" he asked.

They replied, "If today you will be a servant to these people and serve them and give them a favorable answer, they will always be your servants."

"PLANS FAIL FOR LACK OF COUNSEL, BUT WITH MANY ADVISERS THEY SUCCEED" (PROVERBS 15:22).

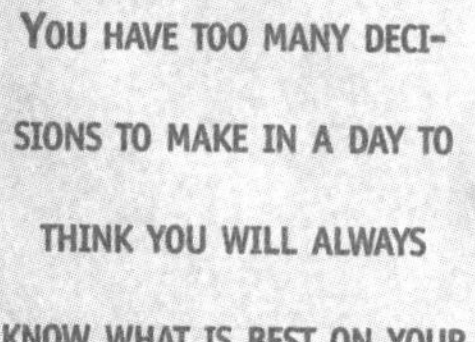

YOU HAVE TOO MANY DECISIONS TO MAKE IN A DAY TO THINK YOU WILL ALWAYS KNOW WHAT IS BEST ON YOUR OWN.

SOME MATTERS DO REQUIRE IMMEDIATE ACTION, BUT NOT EVERYTHING THAT SCREAMS DESERVES AN ABRUPT DECISION. WAITING IS OFTEN THE BEST COURSE OF ACTION.

REHOBOAM LATER REJECTED THE ELDERS' ADVICE IN FAVOR OF HIS FRIENDS' WORDS. COVET THE COMPANY OF WISE ADVISORS.

LEADERSHIP PRINCIPLE NUMBER 64

RESPECT THE OPINIONS OF OTHERS.

I have seen business situations in which no one is willing to tell the top person the bad news he desperately needs to hear. The chief gets only the rosiest of pictures until the bad news becomes so overwhelming it can no longer be hidden. By that time, the battle is often lost and the situation irredeemable.

An executive is only as good as the information he has–both good and bad. You need to be the kind of leader who appreciates and rewards those who will tell you the truth, no matter how distasteful that truth might be.

Jesus continually dismissed insincere flatterers, but accepted honest praise graciously. We need to do the same in all our relationships, but particularly in business. When the rich young ruler came to Jesus calling him "good," Jesus brought him up short because he knew the man was not a sincere worshiper. But when people came with honest praise, he could not have responded more positively.

In business as in life, we need to do as Jesus did: Seek the truth in all things and in all people.

Is This Speaking to You?

Leaning on the advice of others can multiply your skills in using sound judgment. Be humble enough to let them help.

A MATTER OF PRINCIPLE

If your core convictions are firmly in place before times of crisis hit, they will still be standing when the crisis is over.

THE WORD FOR THE DAY

THE FIRST STEP INTO COMPROMISE IS A STEP IN THE WRONG DIRECTION. YOU WILL NEVER REGRET DOING WHAT YOU KNEW WAS RIGHT.

GODLY PRINCIPLES GIVE YOU LIGHT TO SEE IMPORTANT THINGS THAT OTHERS OVERLOOK.

"ABOVE ALL ELSE, GUARD YOUR HEART"—YOUR MOTIVES, YOUR INTENTIONS. THEY REVEAL WHO YOU REALLY ARE, AND DETERMINE THE KIND OF LEADER YOU BECOME.

LOOK AT YOUR LIFE AND LEADERSHIP AS A LONG ROAD, BUT WITH DAILY DECISIONS THAT AFFECT ITS OUTCOME.

PROVERBS 4:13-19, 23-27

Hold on to instruction, do not let it go; guard it well, for it is your life. Do not set foot on the path of the wicked or walk in the way of evil men.

Avoid it, do not travel on it; turn from it and go on your way. For they cannot sleep till they do evil; they are robbed of slumber till they make someone fall. They eat the bread of wickedness and drink the wine of violence.

The path of the righteous is like the first gleam of dawn, shining ever brighter till the full light of day. But the way of the wicked is like deep darkness; they do not know what makes them stumble. . . .

Above all else, guard your heart, for it is the wellspring of life. Put away perversity from your mouth; keep corrupt talk far from your lips.

Let your eyes look straight ahead, fix your gaze directly before you. Make level paths for your feet and take only ways that are firm. Do not swerve to the right or the left; keep your foot from evil.

LEADERSHIP PRINCIPLE NUMBER 65

CHRISTIAN LEADERS OPERATE FROM CLEARLY DEFINED BIBLICAL PRINCIPLES.

From pontificating pundits and tweedy talk show academics who have never met a payroll, we hear that it is not politically correct to insist on absolutes. From truth to justice, all things are relative, they say. It's how you feel about it that counts.

Please don't try to run your business by this nonsense. Jesus insisted that some things are true and others are false, some things are right and others wrong, some things are good and others are evil. He even insisted that there is only one way to be reconciled to God, and that one way is through faith in Him. Talk about tough! Talk about dogmatic! Jesus never equivocated. Sincerity didn't count with Him if what you believed was sincerely wrong.

A lack of absolutes can lead to all kinds of corporate problems, from petty thievery to major crime. It leads to shoddy products and shoddy practices in the marketplace. "I didn't think I was doing anything wrong" is a common defense from people with no rudder to govern their actions. As a company and as a manager, teach the right way, insist on the right way, be an example of the right way.

Is This Speaking to You?

Principle is bigger than burnout, stronger than stress, tougher than temper. Let God's ways rule everything.

GENEROUS HELPINGS

Along with the responsibility of creating and generating comes the blessed responsibility of giving something back.

THE WORD FOR THE DAY

THE CORINTHIANS HAD PLEDGED TO SUPPORT THE JERUSALEM CHURCH BUT HAD BACKED OUT ON THEIR PROMISE. FOLLOW THROUGH ON YOUR COMMITMENTS.

YOUR GENEROSITY HAS EVERYDAY OPPORTUNITIES TO EXPRESS ITSELF. AND LIFELONG REWARDS.

INDIVIDUALS ARE COMMANDED TO TITHE. WHY SHOULDN'T COMPANIES DO THE SAME?

A WATCHING WORLD WANTS TO SEE HOW CHRISTIANS HANDLE THEIR MONEY. DOES YOUR EXAMPLE SHOW THAT MONEY DOESN'T HAVE A HOLD ON YOU?

2 CORINTHIANS 9:6-8, 10-11, 13A

Remember this: Whoever sows sparingly will also reap sparingly, and whoever sows generously will also reap generously.

Each man should give what he has decided in his heart to give, not reluctantly or under compulsion, for God loves a cheerful giver.

And God is able to make all grace abound to you, so that in all things at all times, having all that you need, you will abound in every good work. . . .

Now he who supplies seed to the sower and bread for food will also supply and increase your store of seed and will enlarge the harvest of your righteousness.

You will be made rich in every way so that you can be generous on every occasion, and through us your generosity will result in thanksgiving to God. . . .

Because of the service by which you have proved yourselves, men will praise God for the obedience that accompanies your confession of the gospel of Christ.

LEADERSHIP PRINCIPLE NUMBER 66

LEADERS SHOULD BE GENEROUS WITH THEIR TIME AND MONEY.

In our company, we have sometimes failed to reward one person sufficiently for fear of what some other employee might think. The reasoning goes this way: "If we give Bill the bonus he really deserves, Max will hear about it and be upset that he didn't get a bonus as well."

Max was being paid all that he had been promised and had not performed as exceptionally as Bill. If we were being fair to Max, we shouldn't worry about what he thinks of Bill's compensation. To do so is to cheat Bill out of his rightful reward.

Jesus taught this principle clearly in the parable about the landowner who paid the worker he had hired last (who had worked a much shorter time) the same as those who had worked all day. When confronted about this by one who had worked all day, the landowner replied, "Friend, I am not being unfair to you. . . . I want to give the man who was hired last the same as I gave you. Don't I have the right to do what I want with my own money? Or are you envious because I am so generous?" (Matthew 20:13-15).

Be fair to all. Be generous where generosity is merited.

Is This Speaking to You?

You've worked hard, yet you've been given much to get to this point in leadership. Bless as you've been blessed.

NO COMPROMISE

There are times when taking a short cut in leadership makes so much sense, but is still so much disobedience to God.

THE WORD FOR THE DAY

FROM THE INSTRUCTIONS OF EXODUS 25, THE ARK WAS TO BE CARRIED ON POLES, NOT ON A CART. UZZAH'S DEATH WAS THE RESULT, NOT OF A REFLEX ACTION, BUT AN EARLIER DISOBEDIENCE.

IF YOU WOULDN'T WANT JESUS WATCHING YOU DO IT, DON'T DO IT.

PROCEDURES BECOME OUTDATED, BUT CHANGE THEM ONLY AFTER CAREFUL REVIEW. OTHERS BEFORE YOU MAY HAVE ASKED THE SAME QUESTIONS YOU'RE ASKING NOW, BUT FOUND THE FLAW IN YOUR LOGIC.

"ABSTAIN FROM ALL APPEARANCE OF EVIL" (1 THESSALONIANS 5:22).

2 SAMUEL 6:3-9

They set the ark of God on a new cart and brought it from the house of Abinadab, which was on the hill. Uzzah and Ahio, sons of Abinadab, were guiding the new cart with the ark of God on it, and Ahio was walking in front of it.

David and the whole house of Israel were celebrating with all their might before the LORD, with songs and with harps, lyres, tambourines, sistrums and cymbals.

When they came to the threshing floor of Nacon, Uzzah reached out and took hold of the ark of God, because the oxen stumbled.

The LORD's anger burned against Uzzah because of his irreverent act; therefore God struck him down and he died there beside the ark of God.

Then David was angry because the LORD's wrath had broken out against Uzzah, and to this day that place is called Perez Uzzah.

David was afraid of the LORD that day and said, "How can the ark of the LORD ever come to me?"

Leaders need to know the right way to do things and to practice them. Short cuts or grandstand plays almost never work over time, and when they are substituted for careful execution, people are often hurt.

LEADERSHIP PRINCIPLE NUMBER 67

LEADERS MUST NOT TAKE SHORT CUTS OR BREAK THE RULES EVEN FROM GOOD MOTIVES.

Because oxygen canisters were not loaded properly onto an airline flight, it crashed in the Everglades with great loss of life. Meaning well is never enough. Doing well is the standard.

Uzzah undoubtedly meant well. On the surface he did a useful, helpful, even noble thing. But he did not do the *right* thing, and it cost him his life. In this strange circumstance, brought about because David, the leader, wanted to do things his way, the right thing would have been to let the Ark touch the earth instead of Uzzah's sinful hands.

David assembled thousands of people and had glorious music played in celebration of the Ark's return to Jerusalem. It was a grandstand play. It would have been much better had he quietly followed the instructions and done it right. Enthusiasm must be accompanied by obedience. It is not enough to mean well. We must also do the right thing.

Is This Speaking to You?

Bending a rule may be the only way you see to help you handle your latest problem. But you're only asking for more.

FEAR OF TRYING

When problems pile up faster than you can handle them, that's when leaders make sure they've hidden the panic button.

THE WORD FOR THE DAY

STORMS SPRING UP OFTEN IN THE LEADER'S LIFE, MANY TIMES WITHOUT WARNING. GET YOUR PROBLEM-SOLVING STRATEGIES READY BEFORE THE WORST HITS.

JESUS DIDN'T AVOID THE PROBLEM OR MAKE LIGHT OF HIS FRIENDS' FEARS. HE JUST HANDLED THE SITUATION. LEADERS JUST HANDLE IT.

THERE IS A CALM PLACE IN THE MIDST OF EVERY TRYING SITUATION. AND IT'S NEAR TO THE HEART OF GOD.

FEARFUL SITUATIONS GIVE YOUR FAITH A CHANCE TO PROVE ITS LOFTY WORDS.

MARK 4:35-41

That day when evening came, he said to his disciples, "Let us go over to the other side."

Leaving the crowd behind, they took him along, just as he was, in the boat. There were also other boats with him.

A furious squall came up, and the waves broke over the boat, so that it was nearly swamped.

Jesus was in the stern, sleeping on a cushion. The disciples woke him and said to him, "Teacher, don't you care if we drown?"

He got up, rebuked the wind and said to the waves, "Quiet! Be still!" Then the wind died down and it was completely calm.

He said to his disciples, "Why are you so afraid? Do you still have no faith?"

They were terrified and asked each other, "Who is this? Even the wind and the waves obey him!"

LEADERSHIP PRINCIPLE NUMBER 68

LEADERS ARE NOT FEARLESS, BUT DO NOT LET FEAR DICTATE THEIR THINKING.

Working with live telecasts of major sports events is tantamount to living in the eye of the storm. Many things can go wrong to knock the telecast off the air or cause it to go on at less than its best. The director is the leader and, in a big telecast, has hundreds of followers at his command. If cameras go out, the satellite goes dark, a main power line is severed, or something goes wrong at the network, the director must control the situation by what he says and how he says it. When things start going wrong in a live telecast with millions watching around the world and millions of dollars at stake, a calm leader is a great asset.

I sat in one of our big production trucks at the U.S. Open when things started to go bad, and I saw the director, literally drenched in sweat, keep a voice as calm and reassuring as if he was at his grandmother's house: "Guys, camera three has stopped functioning. We will cover with the overhead until it is back up. Give me some close-ups with that one." No problem. Another day at the office. Everyone remains calm, and the job gets done.

Emulate Jesus' methods. Stay calm when the storm hits.

Is This Speaking to You?

____

____

____

____

____

____

____

____

____

____

____

____

____

____

____

____

____

____

____

____

____

____

You probably have two or three situations swirling around you that need your immediate attention. Act, don't react.

CRITICAL SITUATIONS

It's easy to find fault with those in leadership, but not to find leaders who can find forgiveness in their hearts.

THE WORD FOR THE DAY

IT IS BETTER TO SUFFER UNJUSTLY THAN TO SEEK YOUR OWN REVENGE.

THE BIBLICAL PRINCIPLE OF "SECOND MILE" SERVICE MEANS DOING MORE THAN EXPECTED, WHETHER IT MEANS TAKING A SHORTER LUNCH OR SPORTING A LONGER FUSE.

LEADERSHIP INVITES OPPOSITION. SO WRITE THIS IN STONE AND KEEP IT OUT WHERE YOU CAN ALWAYS REMEMBER IT. "LOVE YOUR ENEMIES."

WORDS FROM PEOPLE YOU DON'T PARTICULARLY LIKE CAN BE HARD TO HEAR. BUT LISTEN ANYWAY. THERE MAY BE SOME TRUTH IN THEM.

MATTHEW 5:38-41, 43-48

"You have heard that it was said, 'Eye for eye, and tooth for tooth.'

"But I tell you, Do not resist an evil person. If someone strikes you on the right cheek, turn to him the other also.

"And if someone wants to sue you and take your tunic, let him have your cloak as well. If someone forces you to go one mile, go with him two miles. . . .

"You have heard that it was said, 'Love your neighbor and hate your enemy.'

"But I tell you: Love your enemies and pray for those who persecute you, that you may be sons of your Father in heaven. He causes his sun to rise on the evil and the good, and sends rain on the righteous and the unrighteous.

"If you love those who love you, what reward will you get? Are not even the tax collectors doing that?

"And if you greet only your brothers, what are you doing more than others? Do not even pagans do that?

"Be perfect, therefore, as your heavenly Father is perfect."

LEADERSHIP PRINCIPLE NUMBER 69

LEADERS KNOW THAT SOME CRITICISM SHOULD BE HEEDED, SOME SHOULD BE IGNORED.

Leadership brings out both the best and the worst in people. Wise leaders understand this, accepting it as a natural part of leadership. They try to emphasize the best and minimize the worst.

Recognize that your motives will always be questioned by some, and that even when you are performing at your very best, creating the most good for the most people, some will take offense. Unfortunately, those offended will often be the people closest to you or those you have known the longest. Just as the people of Nazareth refused to see Jesus as anything other than a carpenter, in spite of the wisdom of His teaching and His miracles of healing, some will never recognize any leadership talent.

When I was a young college baseball coach, my team played exceptionally, and I was named Coach of the Year in my state. One of my oldest friends celebrated my good fortune with me, while another remarked, "Being the best coach in Michigan is no big deal. Michigan is not a college baseball state."

Some celebrate with you. Some don't. This is a reality of leadership. Don't be too surprised by it.

Is This Speaking to You?

If you're under the unkind words of criticism, try not to take it too personally. And try to take it to the Lord first.

YES, YOU WILL

No matter what kind of leadership post you fill, you can hold your staff to a solid work ethic and value system.

THE WORD FOR THE DAY

THE BIBLE MAY OR MAY NOT BE AN ACCEPTED FORM OF AUTHORITY IN YOUR LEADERSHIP ARENA. BUT ITS PRINCIPLES WORK ANYWHERE, WITH ANYBODY.

YOU CAN'T CONTROL THE WAY PEOPLE LIVE WHEN THEY'RE AWAY FROM WORK, BUT YOU CAN DEMAND A HIGH LEVEL OF HONOR AND ACCOUNTABILITY WHEN THEY'RE WITH YOU.

YOUR LOFTY EXPECTATIONS ARE DOING PEOPLE A GREATER SERVICE THAN THEY TRULY REALIZE. NO MATTER HOW MUCH FLAK YOU GET, STAY CONFIDENT YOU'RE DOING WHAT'S BEST FOR THEM.

2 TIMOTHY 2:1-6, 15, 22

You then, my son, be strong in the grace that is in Christ Jesus.

And the things you have heard me say in the presence of many witnesses entrust to reliable men who will also be qualified to teach others.

Endure hardship with us like a good soldier of Christ Jesus.

No one serving as a soldier gets involved in civilian affairs–he wants to please his commanding officer.

Similarly, if anyone competes as an athlete, he does not receive the victor's crown unless he competes according to the rules. The hardworking farmer should be the first to receive a share of the crops. . . .

Do your best to present yourself to God as one approved, a workman who does not need to be ashamed and who correctly handles the word of truth. . . .

Flee the evil desires of youth, and pursue righteousness, faith, love and peace, along with those who call on the Lord out of a pure heart.

LEADERSHIP PRINCIPLE NUMBER 70

LEADERS HAVE A RIGHT TO EXPECT INTEGRITY FROM THE PEOPLE WHO SERVE UNDER THEM.

In business, good management begins with good people. If you hire and hold on to good people, your chances of success go up tremendously. Conversely, incompetent employees will stand in the way of your advancement and success. Unfortunately, building an organization of good people requires both hiring and firing.

The Bible does not say much about hiring and firing employees, but it does say plenty about fairness. As Christians, we are expected to go the extra mile with employees whose performances are not acceptable. An employee, after all, is a person, not a number or a labor unit.

At the same time, however, fairness also means giving truthful evaluations, early warnings, mapping out ways to improve, and then, if the employee does not respond, terminating the relationship with as much grace as possible. In that case, we are being fair to other employees who *are* performing well and to those who have a financial interest in the company. And in terms of our faith, we are communicating the important truth that people of God are people committed to excellence.

Is This Speaking to You?

High standards not only make people better workers, but better people. And isn't that what you're hoping for?

THE LITTLE THINGS

The greatness that people see in you is simply a result of your daily faithfulness. God will always honor that in you.

THE WORD FOR THE DAY

YOUR REACH AND INFLUENCE HAS BEEN ENTRUSTED TO YOU BY GOD. GUARD WELL YOUR CALLING AND THE PEOPLE YOU SERVE WITHIN IT.

DON'T WORRY ABOUT WHAT YOU DON'T HAVE. MAKE THE BEST WITH WHAT YOU DO.

YOU MAY NOT BE IN THE POSITION YOU WANT TO BE, BUT BY SERVING IN IT FAITHFULLY, YOU CAN MAKE THIS A PROFITABLE SEASON OF LIFE.

YES, DO THE LITTLE THINGS WELL, BUT DON'T LET YOUR LARGER VISION GET BOGGED DOWN IN THE DETAILS.

MATTHEW 25:14-21

"Again, it will be like a man going on a journey, who called his servants and entrusted his property to them.

"To one he gave five talents of money, to another two talents, and to another one talent, each according to his ability. Then he went on his journey.

"The man who had received the five talents went at once and put his money to work and gained five more. So also, the one with the two talents gained two more. But the man who had received the one talent went off, dug a hole in the ground and hid his master's money.

"After a long time the master of those servants returned and settled accounts with them. The man who had received the five talents brought the other five. 'Master,' he said, 'you entrusted me with five talents. See, I have gained five more.'

"His master replied, 'Well done, good and faithful servant! You have been faithful with a few things; I will put you in charge of many things. Come and share your master's happiness!' "

LEADERSHIP PRINCIPLE NUMBER 71

DO THE LITTLE THINGS WELL.

Leaders must understand that little things do mean a lot and that everything they do is magnified in the minds of those they lead. Every word, gesture, smile, or frown takes on added significance when it comes from a leader. A follower's day can be ruined without a word of greeting from his or her leader. Conversely, a follower can be inspired and energized by the slightest positive comment from a leader.

General Eisenhower spent the last few hours before D-Day, not mingling with the top brass but with the soldiers, sailors, and airmen who were about to invade Europe. Don't become so preoccupied with thoughts of leadership that you fail to plant the mustard seed that will grow into a great, worthwhile relationship between you and those you lead. Be sensitive. Be alert.

The Bible often celebrates small things. It was little David, not the giant Goliath. It was Gideon's small band, not the enemy hordes. It was the widow's mite, not the Pharisee's showy appearances. It was the cup of cold water, not the grandstand play. Sometimes it's better to think small.

Is This Speaking to You?

If you're saving your best efforts for the next big thing, you'll miss a lot of opportunities to prepare yourself for it.

DAY SEVENTY-TWO

OUTSIDE THE BOX

Some days you wish you could just go through the motions and fill in the blanks. But you've been called higher than that.

THE WORD FOR THE DAY

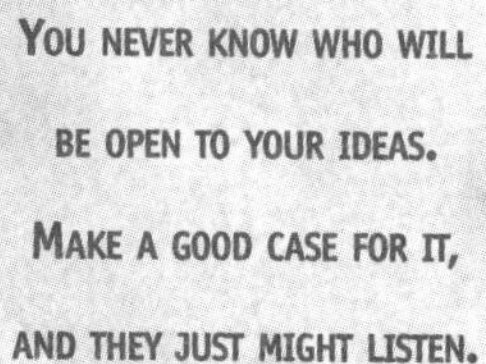

CHALLENGE THE RUT OF UNQUESTIONED EXPECTATIONS WITH THE FRESH AIR OF A NEW APPROACH.

YOU NEVER KNOW WHO WILL BE OPEN TO YOUR IDEAS. MAKE A GOOD CASE FOR IT, AND THEY JUST MIGHT LISTEN.

TV AND TALK SHOWS ASK NOTHING OF YOUR BRAIN. CHOOSE RECREATIONAL ACTIVITIES THAT CHANGE YOUR PACE, BUT STIMULATE YOUR MIND.

DON'T BE AFRAID TO ACT ON YOUR HUNCHES.

TWEAKS AND ADJUSTMENTS ALONG THE WAY CAN AVOID YOUR NEED FOR A TOTAL OVERHAUL.

NUMBERS 27:1-8

The daughters of Zelophehad . . . belonged to the clans of Manasseh son of Joseph. The names of the daughters were Mahlah, Noah, Hoglah, Milcah and Tirzah.

They approached the entrance to the Tent of Meeting and stood before Moses, Eleazar the priest, the leaders and the whole assembly, and said,

"Our father died in the desert. He was not among Korah's followers, who banded together against the LORD, but he died for his own sin and left no sons. Why should our father's name disappear from his clan because he had no son? Give us property among our father's relatives."

So Moses brought their case before the LORD and the LORD said to him, "What Zelophehad's daughters are saying is right. You must certainly give them property as an inheritance among their father's relatives and give their father's inheritance over to them.

"Say to the Israelites, 'If a man dies and leaves no son, give his inheritance over to his daughter.'"

LEADERSHIP PRINCIPLE NUMBER 72

LEADERS MUST THINK CREATIVELY, BEYOND THE ORDINARY AND EXPECTED.

Leaders should constantly keep before them three very important questions. The first is: "Am I willing to really lead?" When those who have leadership roles refuse to lead, decisions aren't made and communicated. Roles aren't defined. Assignments are not clearly given. Discipline is not maintained. Order is not kept, and direction is lost. Leaders must lead.

The second questions is: "Am I willing to think of new ways of doing things?" *If it's not broke, don't fix it* is not a motto for leaders. A leader should see every enterprise as broken enough to ask how it can be done better, more efficiently, more beneficially. This is what leadership is all about. Managers accept things as they are. Leaders do not.

The third question is: "Am I willing to be open and vulnerable enough with a core group of followers that I can share bad news with them in a timely way?" This is the way Jesus led. He continually told His disciples both about the coming kingdom and the terribly high cost of bringing it about. This is a lesson for all leaders.

As you lead and consider leading, ask yourself these questions.

Is This Speaking to You?

God can give you an understanding of the past, but His vision is for the future. Ask for His help in thinking ahead.

HIGH-MINDED

You should have a lot more in your sights than the next big deadline. Looking back, it won't seem quite so important.

THE WORD FOR THE DAY

THE PROBLEMS AND ISSUES YOU FACED TEN YEARS AGO SEEM SMALL TO YOU NOW. IMAGINE HOW SMALL TODAY'S WILL SEEM . . . FOREVER FROM NOW.

DON'T MAKE GOD HAVE TO TAKE SOMETHING FROM YOU BEFORE YOU REALIZE HOW VALUABLE IT IS.

THE TRAITS OF AN ETERNITY-MINDED PERSON ARE LOVE, PATIENCE, FORGIVENESS, PEACEFULNESS, GRATITUDE. ALL THE GOOD THINGS.

"YES, I AM COMING SOON.' AMEN. COME, LORD JESUS" (REVELATION 22:20).

COLOSSIANS 3:1-4, 12-15

Since, then, you have been raised with Christ, set your hearts on things above, where Christ is seated at the right hand of God.

Set your minds on things above, not on earthly things. For you died, and your life is now hidden with Christ in God. When Christ, who is your life, appears, then you also will appear with him in glory. . . .

Therefore, as God's chosen people, holy and dearly loved, clothe yourselves with compassion, kindness, humility, gentleness and patience.

Bear with each other and forgive whatever grievances you may have against one another. Forgive as the Lord forgave you.

And over all these virtues put on love, which binds them all together in perfect unity.

Let the peace of Christ rule in your hearts, since as members of one body you were called to peace. And be thankful.

LEADERSHIP PRINCIPLE NUMBER 73

SUCCESSFUL LEADERS VIEW THEIR TASKS FROM AN ETERNAL PERSPECTIVE.

Jesus had a lot on His mind. He must have been looking ahead to those final few days in Jerusalem when He would enter as king to the cheers of the crowd, only to be crucified with two thieves five days later. No one could blame Him if He simply didn't have the time to bother with a blind man in Jericho. But Jesus stopped and took the time to heal him.

Ponder that thought for a moment. This picture of Jesus summarizes just about everything about leadership. Leaders are the people who show the way because they have a clear sense of where they are going. They walk into the future with courage and challenge others to follow them. They are often misunderstood and sometimes bitterly opposed. They stay focused on the things that matter, but they never forget that people matter more than things. They fight tenaciously for what they believe because they believe in a cause bigger than themselves. That cause consumes them and becomes the rallying point for everyone who follows them.

While you're on your way to the top, keep your eyes on a future that's even brighter.

Is This Speaking to You?

It seems trite, but it's just so true. Try to view this day with the perspective that you may not get this chance again.

ENCOURAGING WORDS

Some people are able to rise to a challenge. But everyone stands a little taller when they feel genuinely appreciated.

THE WORD FOR THE DAY

PAUL'S LETTERS ALMOST ALWAYS BEGIN WITH AN ENCOURAGING WORD. THERE'S ALWAYS SOMETHING GOOD YOU CAN SAY.

LETTERS, NOTES, AND CARDS CAN TOUCH THE HEART EVEN MORE THAN THE SPOKEN WORD.

PRAYER AND ENCOURAGEMENT OFTEN GO TOGETHER. WHEN YOU TELL SOMEONE YOU'RE PRAYING FOR THEM, MAKE SURE YOU DO.

THE ULTIMATE GOAL OF PAUL'S ENCOURAGEMENT WAS TO HELP PEOPLE WANT TO LIVE HOLY LIVES FOR THE LORD.

1 THESSALONIANS 3:6-12

Timothy has just now come to us from you and has brought good news about your faith and love. He has told us that you always have pleasant memories of us and that you long to see us, just as we also long to see you.

Therefore, brothers, in all our distress and persecution we were encouraged about you because of your faith.

For now we really live, since you are standing firm in the Lord.

How can we thank God enough for you in return for all the joy we have in the presence of our God because of you?

Night and day we pray most earnestly that we may see you again and supply what is lacking in your faith.

Now may our God and Father himself and our Lord Jesus clear the way for us to come to you. May the Lord make your love increase and overflow for each other and for everyone else, just as ours does for you.

LEADERSHIP PRINCIPLE NUMBER 74

LEADERS WHO ARE MOTIVATED TO ENCOURAGE OTHERS ARE THE ONES WHO MOTIVATE THE BEST.

When you consider how many things of paramount importance were conveyed by Jesus to His disciples while they were eating, it is impossible not to note the significance of food and mealtimes in the building of His organization.

Sharing meals together creates a special atmosphere for building relationships. The Last Supper is the most obvious example of this, but it is not the only one. On many occasions, mealtime was special in Jesus' work with His disciples. These were particularly important times of sharing His thoughts and vision. Eating with His disciples helped Him do that.

Managers neglect these lessons to their detriment. There is a temptation to have lunch at your desk in order to move more paper, to eat with a customer to increase sales, or to eat with your peers from other companies for fun and fellowship. There is nothing wrong with any of these options, and they should be part of a well-considered schedule. But meals with those who work with you and for you should also be a part of that schedule.

Eat with your troops. It will make them better soldiers.

Is This Speaking to You?

You may have to go out of your way to give someone an encouraging word. But it'll be worth every step you take.

AGREE TO DISAGREE

After knocking heads together enough times, there are certain situations where the best path is to part paths.

THE WORD FOR THE DAY

The Bible helps us remember that these people were only human. Who can't relate to having "such a sharp disagreement?"

Separation should be a last resort. First, seek common ground.

It is a faulty expectation that believers will always get along with each other. Conflict shouldn't be a surprise.

Paul and Barnabas later worked together again. And John Mark finally regained Paul's confidence. Goodbyes are not forever. Don't burn your bridges along the way.

ACTS 15:36-41
MATTHEW 10:34-36

Some time later Paul said to Barnabas, "Let us go back and visit the brothers in all the towns where we preached the word of the Lord and see how they are doing."

Barnabas wanted to take John, also called Mark, with them, but Paul did not think it wise to take him, because he had deserted them in Pamphylia and had not continued with them in the work.

They had such a sharp disagreement that they parted company. Barnabas took Mark and sailed for Cyprus, but Paul chose Silas and left, commended by the brothers to the grace of the Lord.

He went through Syria and Cilicia, strengthening the churches. . . .

"Do not suppose that I have come to bring peace to the earth. I did not come to bring peace, but a sword.

"For I have come to turn 'a man against his father, a daughter against her mother, a daughter-in-law against her mother-in-law– a man's enemies will be the members of his own household.'"

There are many lessons to be learned from this incident, and we can be very thankful that Luke, led by the Holy Spirit, included it in his writing of Acts. In fact, scholars tell us that the recording of this rather unpleasant incident helps to authenticate the book of Acts. It shows that it is not just a propaganda piece for the new Christian faith, but is an accurate historical account of what happened in the early days of the church.

Among the most important leadership lessons it teaches is that when your mission is clear and well defined, it can be accomplished in a number of ways. In fact, their mission was advanced rather than retarded by this disagreement. The argument brought about two strong teams instead of one. When we are clear about our mission and obedient to God's direction, good things can result from bad situations.

Wise leaders also understand that life is a long race with many twists and turns. Be very slow to write people off. Down the road, we may want to work again with people we once disagreed with. The old adage about not burning bridges is a good one.

LEADERSHIP PRINCIPLE NUMBER 75

WHEN SHARP DISAGREEMENTS OCCUR AMONG LEADERS, IT IS OFTEN BETTER TO PART COMPANY.

Is This Speaking to You?

Some things are worth fighting for. Some things are not. Ask God to help you know how to tell the difference.

CLEARING THE ERROR

Part of working with people is being hurt by them. But to play your part as a leader, you must be the first to forgive.

THE WORD FOR THE DAY

WATCH JOSEPH'S BROTHERS RETURN TO THEIR TRICKERY. EVEN IN FORGIVING, YOU MAY NEED TO WITHHOLD YOUR TRUST, AT LEAST FOR A WHILE.

MOST DISAGREEMENTS ARE MISUNDERSTANDINGS THAT STEM FROM PRIVATE, UNRELATED PROBLEMS. BEFORE YOU REACT, TRY FIRST TO SEE THE MOTIVE BEHIND THE BEHAVIOR.

PETTY MATTERS CAN ASSUME GIGANTIC PROPORTIONS. SETTLE LITTLE ISSUES BEFORE THEY SIDETRACK YOUR VISION.

"A GENTLE ANSWER TURNS AWAY WRATH, BUT A HARSH WORD STIRS UP ANGER" (PROVERBS 15:1).

GENESIS 50:15-21

When Joseph's brothers saw that their father was dead, they said, "What if Joseph holds a grudge against us and pays us back for all the wrongs we did to him?"

So they sent word to Joseph, saying, "Your father left these instructions before he died: 'This is what you are to say to Joseph: I ask you to forgive your brothers the sins and the wrongs they committed in treating you so badly.' Now please forgive the sins of the servants of the God of your father." When their message came to him, Joseph wept.

His brothers then came and threw themselves down before him. "We are your slaves," they said.

But Joseph said to them, "Don't be afraid. Am I in the place of God? You intended to harm me, but God intended it for good to accomplish what is now being done, the saving of many lives.

"So then, don't be afraid. I will provide for you and your children." And he reassured them and spoke kindly to them.

LEADERSHIP PRINCIPLE NUMBER 76

LEADERS MUST BE QUICK TO ASK FOR FORGIVENESS, EVEN QUICKER TO GIVE IT.

One of the great tensions for a leader–especially a Christian leader–is the delicate balance between accountability and forgiveness. We should expect and demand a high level of integrity and performance in our employees. But we must be willing to forgive them when they fail in their duties, if we are to be like Jesus.

This does not mean that we should look the other way when mistakes are made. Quite the contrary, it means we must address breakdowns in character and offer the right response or counter-measure to correct the situation.

Do you think that the forgiveness which we receive from God means that He is ignoring our sin or sweeping it under the rug? Absolutely not. He has dealt with our sin by offering the blood of His Son as the only suitable sacrifice. He has not taken lightly the wrong things we have done, but has gone to great lengths to help us correct our fatal problem.

There are times when the dismissal of an employee is the most redemptive thing you can do for him. But God still expects us to forgive him in our heart.

Is This Speaking to You?

It's terrible to have people you feel the need to avoid because of unresolved conflict. Talk about it. Get it out in the open.

LEADERSHIP COSTS

People see your name on the program, your picture in the paper. If they could only see what goes on behind the scenes.

THE WORD FOR THE DAY

MOSES BEING PUNISHED? AFTER ONE LITTLE SLIP-UP? LEADERSHIP COMES WITH GRAVE RESPONSIBILITIES . . . AND THE WILLINGNESS TO SEE THIS AS BEING FAIR.

BE CAREFUL OF WHAT YOU DEMAND AS YOUR RIGHTS. EXPECT TO WORK HARDER THAN ANYONE WHO ANSWERS TO YOU.

WORK HARD TO MAKE SURE THAT YOUR FAMILY AND CHILDREN AREN'T THE ONES PAYING THE BIGGEST PRICE FOR YOUR OUTSIDE COMMITMENTS.

OTHERS ARE WATCHING TO SEE HOW YOU HANDLE YOUR STRESSES. IS GOD PLEASED BY WHAT THEY SEE?

NUMBERS 20:2, 7-12

Now there was no water for the community, and the people gathered in opposition to Moses and Aaron. . . .

The LORD said to Moses, "Take the staff, and you and your brother Aaron gather the assembly together. Speak to that rock before their eyes and it will pour out its water. You will bring water out of the rock for the community so that they and their livestock can drink."

So Moses took the staff from the LORD's presence, just as he commanded him.

He and Aaron gathered the assembly together in front of the rock and Moses said to them, "Listen, you rebels, must we bring you water out of this rock?"

Then Moses raised his arm and struck the rock twice with his staff. Water gushed out, and the community and their livestock drank.

But the LORD said to Moses and Aaron, "Because you did not trust in me enough to honor me as holy in the sight of the Israelites, you will not bring this community into the land I give them."

LEADERSHIP PRINCIPLE NUMBER 77

LEADERS ENJOY GREAT PRIVILEGES, BUT THEY PAY A HIGHER PRICE.

A leader is disciplined. If you expect discipline among your followers and lack it in your own life, your followers will first lose respect and then grow to resent you.

Mark was very precise in saying, "Very early in the morning, while it was still dark, Jesus got up, left the house and went off to a solitary place, where he prayed" (Mark 1:35). Jesus disciplined himself in the wise use of time. He was up and at 'em early. More importantly, however, he disciplined himself to a time of prayer and solitude–prerequisites for Christians to succeed in any kind of leadership position.

Finding time for both is not an option but a requirement. A habit of prayer is perhaps more easily developed than a habit of solitude. Leaders can pray at a variety of times, but solitude must be sought diligently. Although the nature of a leader-follower relationship requires some degree of togetherness, a leader must discipline himself to establish time apart from the team. Great leaders, from Abraham Lincoln to Winston Churchill to Thomas Edison, followed Jesus' example of setting aside quiet time alone. So should you.

Is This Speaking to You?

Let the rest of the world sleep in on Saturdays and waste their talents on meaningless trivia. You have a job to do.

NO NEED TO THANK ME

You may have to go weeks and months between compliments, but you can live off God's seal of approval any day.

THE WORD FOR THE DAY

WHETHER EVERYONE SEES OR NO ONE SEES, YOUR WORK HAS VALUE THAT GOD CAN SEE.

TOO MUCH IS MADE OF TITLES AND ACCOMPLISHMENTS. WE ARE VALUED "NOT BECAUSE OF ANYTHING WE HAVE DONE, BUT BECAUSE OF HIS OWN PURPOSE AND GRACE."

WHETHER AT WORK IN THE TRENCHES OR CONFINED IN PRISON, PAUL KNEW THAT GOD WAS THE ONE BRINGING ABOUT THE RESULTS.

YOU CAN'T DEPEND ON ENCOURAGEMENT, BUT YOU CAN'T LEAD WITHOUT GIVING IT.

2 TIMOTHY 1:8-12, 14

So do not be ashamed to testify about our Lord, or ashamed of me his prisoner. But join with me in suffering for the gospel, by the power of God, who has saved us and called us to a holy life–not because of anything we have done but because of his own purpose and grace.

This grace was given us in Christ Jesus before the beginning of time, but it has now been revealed through the appearing of our Savior, Christ Jesus, who has destroyed death and has brought life and immortality to light through the gospel.

And of this gospel I was appointed a herald and an apostle and a teacher. That is why I am suffering as I am. Yet I am not ashamed, because I know whom I have believed, and am convinced that he is able to guard what I have entrusted to him for that day. . . .

Guard the good deposit that was entrusted to you–guard it with the help of the Holy Spirit who lives in us.

LEADERSHIP PRINCIPLE NUMBER 78

LEADERS DON'T NEED CONSTANT APPROVAL TO VALIDATE THEIR WORK.

Jesus showed us that even when we work exclusively for the welfare of others, some may say we are evil. In His case, the Pharisees deliberately twisted His words and deeds to make them appear self-serving and blasphemous. The apostle Paul also was maligned and mistreated during his years of ministry, though he was simply living out the mission God had called him to fulfill.

The same thing happens to leaders today, even to those with the best motives and the highest standards. You will never be fairly judged at all times. It is possible to do nothing but good and *still* be attacked. Don't expect fairness in a fallen world.

Winston Churchill was perhaps the greatest leader of the twentieth century. His magnificent, courageous leadership of the British people during the darkest days of World War II inspired freedom-loving people everywhere. Yet in the first election after his leadership helped to secure victory over the Nazis, he was immediately voted out of office! This is an example of what leaders often face. Universal appreciation doesn't always follow great leadership.

Is This Speaking to You?

The correct posture of the Christian is neither haughtiness nor false humility, but a calm assurance of your role in God's plan.

WORK IN PROGRESS

The fruits of your labors will only taste as sweet as the grateful attitude you've used in completing your work.

THE WORD FOR THE DAY

NOAH HAD GOOD HELP AND THE APPROVAL OF GOD DURING HIS 100-YEAR BOAT PROJECT, BUT EVEN THESE BLESSINGS DIDN'T NEGATE HIS NEED FOR HARD WORK.

"HE WHO WORKS HIS LAND WILL HAVE ABUNDANT FOOD, BUT HE WHO CHASES FANTASIES LACKS JUDGMENT" (PROVERBS 12:11).

CHECK REGULARLY TO BE SURE YOUR HARD WORK IS AS PRODUCTIVE AS IT IS DILIGENT.

"NOAH DID EVERYTHING JUST AS GOD COMMANDED HIM." THIS SHOULD BE THE HEARTBEAT OF EVERY CHRISTIAN LEADER.

GENESIS 6:13-16, 19-22

So God said to Noah, "I am going to put an end to all people, for the earth is filled with violence because of them. I am surely going to destroy both them and the earth.

"So make yourself an ark of cypress wood; make rooms in it and coat it with pitch inside and out. This is how you are to build it: The ark is to be 450 feet long, 75 feet wide and 45 feet high.

"Make a roof for it and finish the ark to within 18 inches of the top. Put a door in the side of the ark and make lower, middle and upper decks. . . ."

"You are to bring into the ark two of all living creatures, male and female, to keep them alive with you. Two of every kind of bird, of every kind of animal and of every kind of creature that moves along the ground will come to you to be kept alive. You are to take every kind of food that is to be eaten and store it away as food for you and for them."

Noah did everything just as God commanded him.

LEADERSHIP PRINCIPLE NUMBER 79

SOUND LEADERSHIP REQUIRES MORE THAN HARD WORK, BUT IT WILL NOT HAPPEN WITHOUT IT.

Every day you face a choice of going one of two ways–the easy way or the hard way. The easy way is the way of procrastination, of staying in bed when the alarm goes off, of saying it doesn't matter whether I work today or not. It doesn't matter what time I show up or if I check out a few minutes early. The boss isn't around. It's close enough for government work. It is the way of no plans, no forethought, no enthusiasm, no diligence.

Many people talk about doing something–writing a book, starting a company, beginning a ministry–but few actually do the hard work of getting it done. As the old saying goes, "When all is said and done, more is said than done." Real leaders are not fantasizers and talkers, they are doers. They work hard.

The hard road, which appears to be so difficult, is ultimately the road of blessing, fulfillment, and lasting spiritual growth. It is the road that leads you to the top, and it is the road that allows you to take others along with you.

Work hard. The rewards are many for you and for those who follow you.

Is This Speaking to You?

You can expect a reward from all your hard work–not by how much you've done, but by how well you've done it.

CHECK YOUR CALENDAR

Your day planner can quickly get to be a real handful. But how'd you like to get a better grip on your time?

THE WORD FOR THE DAY

DON'T LET YOUR PAST FAILINGS BE A SOURCE OF GUILT AND FRUSTRATION, BUT A CHALLENGE TO MAKE EVERY REMAINING MINUTE COUNT.

IN MANAGING YOUR TIME, BE SURE TO MAINTAIN A BALANCE BETWEEN FAMILY, WORK, HOME, AND MINISTRY.

UP EARLY, TO BED LATE. A GOOD NIGHT'S SLEEP SHOULD NOT BE A CONSTANT CASUALTY OF YOUR BUSY SCHEDULE.

BEING IDLE IS PROBABLY NOT YOUR PROBLEM. BUT CHOOSE ACTIVITIES CAREFULLY FOR THE SPARE TIME YOU DO HAVE.

EPHESIANS 5:1-2, 8-16

Be imitators of God, therefore, as dearly loved children and live a life of love, just as Christ loved us and gave himself up for us as a fragrant offering and sacrifice to God. . . .

For you were once darkness, but now you are light in the Lord. Live as children of light (for the fruit of the light consists in all goodness, righteousness and truth) and find out what pleases the Lord.

Have nothing to do with the fruitless deeds of darkness, but rather expose them. For it is shameful even to mention what the disobedient do in secret.

But everything exposed by the light becomes visible, for it is light that makes everything visible. This is why it is said: "Wake up, O sleeper, rise from the dead, and Christ will shine on you."

Be very careful, then, how you live–not as unwise but as wise, making the most of every opportunity, because the days are evil.

LEADERSHIP PRINCIPLE NUMBER 80

THE WAY YOU MANAGE YOUR TIME REFLECTS WHAT'S REALLY IMPORTANT TO YOU.

Wise leaders always have a schedule, a plan to use their time most productively, but the wisest leader never makes it his master.

Important but unplanned moments periodically occur that should not be lost, even though they disrupt a planned schedule. One of the tensions of leadership is finding the proper balance between adhering to a well-planned schedule and being flexible enough not to lose those spontaneous opportunities that cross our paths.

How do we find balance? Jesus had a plan, which He pursued relentlessly to accomplish. But as He did so, he utilized those special, unplanned occasions to contribute to the successful conclusion of His original plan.

Compassion was the motivation that usually caused Jesus to deviate from His schedule. That may not seem useful for today's leaders, but consider this: a concern for the welfare of people rarely leads us to an unprofitable or unproductive use of our time. Wise compassion is a clear-headed emotion that enables us to strive to accomplish the most good for the most people. And isn't that what leadership is all about?

Is This Speaking to You?

If you never feel like you're accomplishing enough, maybe it's because you're trying to do too much.

THE REAL WORLD

It would be nice if we didn't have to worry about the larger issues of our culture. But that wouldn't be leadership.

THE WORD FOR THE DAY

OUR KINGDOM IS NOT OF THIS WORLD, BUT WE HAVE A RESPONSIBILITY TO ITS PEOPLE, TO WORK FOR THEIR GOOD, TO FIGHT FOR THEIR SOULS.

UNDERSTANDING THE TIMES CAN HELP YOU KEEP YOUR VISION IN TUNE WITH THE REAL NEEDS AROUND YOU.

YOU'LL PROBABLY LEARN MORE FROM LISTENING TO PEOPLE THAN FROM READING MAGAZINES AND WATCHING THE HEADLINES.

WITH SO MUCH INFORMATION AVAILABLE, YOU MUST ASK GOD TO HELP DISCERN THE THINGS YOU TRULY NEED TO KNOW.

2 TIMOTHY 3:1-5, 12-15

But mark this: There will be terrible times in the last days.

People will be lovers of themselves, lovers of money, boastful, proud, abusive, disobedient to their parents, ungrateful, unholy, without love, unforgiving, slanderous, without self-control, brutal, not lovers of the good, treacherous, rash, conceited, lovers of pleasure rather than lovers of God–having a form of godliness but denying its power. Have nothing to do with them. . . .

In fact, everyone who wants to live a godly life in Christ Jesus will be persecuted, while evil men and impostors will go from bad to worse, deceiving and being deceived.

But as for you, continue in what you have learned and have become convinced of, because you know those from whom you learned it, and how from infancy you have known the holy Scriptures, which are able to make you wise for salvation through faith in Christ Jesus.

LEADERSHIP PRINCIPLE NUMBER 81

GOOD LEADERS POSSESS A BROAD UNDERSTANDING OF THE TIMES IN WHICH THEY LIVE.

Men and women with the gift of leadership have insight into the purposes of God. They are able to look into the future and see what God wants done. They see the forest when everyone else sees problems.

This is perhaps our greatest need today–for leaders with insight who understand the times in which we live and understand how best to influence them for God and his Kingdom. Today, we see Christian leaders reacting to the times in all sorts of ways, some which are productive and some which are not. Some leaders call for a complete retreat from the culture. Some call for a frontal attack with boycotts and protests. Some lead political movements as a way to influence the culture.

Surely, the way to influence the culture is by being obedient to the commands of Scripture. If we are to be the salt that Jesus admonishes us to be, we must proclaim the gospel and make disciples as he commands us. Leaders who lead us into obedience in these areas will be serving both the church and the nation. Seeing the times through the lens of Scripture produces the best understanding, and obedience produces the best results.

Is This Speaking to You?

The newscasts are cutting edge, but the Bible continues to speak to this age. Ask God to let it speak to you clearly.

SEEING THE CHANGE

Imagine a world where everything always stays the same, because that's the only place where a world like that exists.

THE WORD FOR THE DAY

CHANGE CAN BE AS SCARY AS A MURDEROUS SAUL MUST HAVE SEEMED TO THE EARLY CHURCH. BUT GOOD THINGS CAN COME AS A RESULT OF IT.

IMPROVE YOUR OWN LEADERSHIP ABILITY BY STRIVING TO STAY ONE STEP AHEAD OF THE CHANGE CYCLES.

BUT EVEN IN TIMES OF CHANGE, YOU SHOULD POSSESS SOME THINGS THAT *NEVER* CHANGE—VALUES YOU'D DEFEND NO MATTER WHAT.

THE BEST LEADERSHIP STYLES MIX THE OLD WITH THE NEW, STAYING CURRENT WITHOUT BECOMING RUDDERLESS.

ACTS 9:19B-22, 26-28

Saul spent several days with the disciples in Damascus. At once he began to preach in the synagogues that Jesus is the Son of God.

All those who heard him were astonished and asked, "Isn't he the man who caused havoc in Jerusalem among those who call on this name? And hasn't he come here to take them as prisoners to the chief priests?"

Yet Saul grew more and more powerful and baffled the Jews living in Damascus by proving that Jesus is the Christ. . . .

When he came to Jerusalem, he tried to join the disciples, but they were all afraid of him, not believing that he really was a disciple.

But Barnabas took him and brought him to the apostles. He told them how Saul on his journey had seen the Lord and that the Lord had spoken to him, and how in Damascus he had preached fearlessly in the name of Jesus.

So Saul stayed with them and moved about freely in Jerusalem, speaking boldly in the name of the Lord.

LEADERSHIP PRINCIPLE NUMBER 82

A NEW DAY OFTEN CALLS FOR A NEW STRATEGY, A NEW SHAPE, A WHOLE NEW APPROACH.

Among the most important abilities a leader must cultivate is that of discerning between essential core issues and those that might seem to be important, but really are only packaging. It is particularly important for Christian leaders to be sure they understand what Os Guiness calls the "first things of the gospel"–who Jesus is and why He came–and to keep the focus of their leadership there. All the rest is essentially packaging.

However, packaging is important, whether we are talking about business or about spreading the Gospel. It is not the *most* important, but it does help determine the degree of success we will have. We need to be sure we preserve the core, and then package it in the most advantageous, productive, and protective way.

It is sad to see churches split over packaging issues such as style of worship. The best leadership keeps that from happening. Leadership preserves the essential core while making sure that packaging considerations are dealt with in timely, objective, and dispassionate ways.

Is This Speaking to You?

When changes have upset your world, try to remember that God has seen it all before. And lived to tell about it.

LIFELONG LEARNING

Leaders love to teach, to motivate, to inform. But it all goes back to a love even deeper than these–a love of learning.

THE WORD FOR THE DAY

LEARNING IS WHAT LEADERS DO WHILE THE REST OF THE WORLD IS WATCHING TV AND READING CEREAL BOXES.

THERE'S A LOT OF SO-CALLED WISDOM OUT THERE THAT EVEN TALKS ABOUT A SO-CALLED GOD. BE SURE YOUR ADOPTED TRUTHS COME FROM THE ONE TRUE AUTHOR.

YOU CAN'T LIVE ON BORROWED KNOWLEDGE. READING AND FIRSTHAND OBSERVATION WILL MAKE WISDOM YOURS.

"WISDOM IS SUPREME; THEREFORE GET WISDOM. THOUGH IT COST ALL YOU HAVE, GET UNDERSTANDING" (PROVERBS 4:7).

1 KINGS 10:1-3, 6-8

When the queen of Sheba heard about the fame of Solomon and his relation to the name of the LORD, she came to test him with hard questions.

Arriving at Jerusalem with a very great caravan–with camels carrying spices, large quantities of gold, and precious stones–she came to Solomon and talked with him about all that she had on her mind.

Solomon answered all her questions; nothing was too hard for the king to explain to her. . . .

She said to the king, "The report I heard in my own country about your achievements and your wisdom is true.

"But I did not believe these things until I came and saw with my own eyes. Indeed, not even half was told me; in wisdom and wealth you have far exceeded the report I heard.

"How happy your men must be! How happy your officials, who continually stand before you and hear your wisdom!"

It's time for the lambs to roar.

What I'm calling for is a radically different way of thinking about our world. Instead of running from it, we need to rush into it. And instead of just hanging around the fringes of our culture, we need to be right smack dab in the middle of it.

LEADERSHIP PRINCIPLE NUMBER 83

LEADERS NEVER STOP LEARNING.

The church, like so many others, is filled with lambs who've lost their voice. Not only have they failed to penetrate their community with their values, they have come to accept failure as inevitable. But it is time for us to start thinking about what this faith of ours is supposed to do and to mean. We must learn how to engage our culture and demonstrate the truths of God.

I believe it's not only possible but absolutely necessary for Christians and Christian values to become a vital element in the overall moral and cultural discourse of our nation. Without our strategic involvement in the culture-shaping arenas of art, entertainment, the media, education, and the like, this nation cannot be the great and glorious society it once was. We need to learn how to re-enter the fields that we have fled.

Are you ready to roar?

Is This Speaking to You?

The desire is already there. The challenge is clearing some spots in your week where learning can become a habit.

PEOPLE MATTER MOST

We all deal with certain people who can get under our skin. But no one in our lives should be beneath our dignity.

THE WORD FOR THE DAY

ADD TO YOUR LIST OF TALENTS AND ACCOMPLISHMENTS THE ABILITY TO BE BIGGER THAN OTHER'S DIFFERENCES.

"NO ONE HAS EVER SEEN GOD, BUT IF WE LOVE ONE ANOTHER, GOD LIVES IN US AND HIS LOVE IS MADE COMPLETE IN US"

(1 JOHN 4:12).

YOU DON'T HAVE TO LIKE SOMEONE TO WANT THE BEST FOR THEM, AND TO WORK FOR THEIR GOOD EVEN WHEN THEY'VE BEEN A PROBLEM.

THE TIME MAY COME FOR YOU TO DISMISS SOMEONE FROM YOUR WORK FORCE, BUT NEVER FROM YOUR PRAYER LIST.

1 CORINTHIANS 12:31-13:8, 13

And now I will show you the most excellent way.

If I speak in the tongues of men and of angels, but have not love, I am only a resounding gong or a clanging cymbal.

If I have the gift of prophecy and can fathom all mysteries and all knowledge, and if I have a faith that can move mountains, but have not love, I am nothing.

If I give all I possess to the poor and surrender my body to the flames, but have not love, I gain nothing.

Love is patient, love is kind. It does not envy, it does not boast, it is not proud.

It is not rude, it is not self-seeking, it is not easily angered, it keeps no record of wrongs.

Love does not delight in evil but rejoices with the truth. It always protects, always trusts, always hopes, always perseveres.

Love never fails. . . .

And now these three remain: faith, hope and love. But the greatest of these is love.

LEADERSHIP PRINCIPLE NUMBER 84

PEOPLE ARE NOT EXPENDABLE.

Jesus constantly evaluated His disciples. He wanted to see if they were really grasping all that He was trying to teach them. He did this by staying involved with them and by asking them questions. But most often He was disappointed with their answers and found that He had more teaching to do.

Don't take communication with others for granted, especially those who are the most difficult to motivate. Make sure that those working for you understand both the company's goals and the methods to reach those goals. Managers often assume that everyone is on the same page and that everyone agrees on both the goals and the ways to reach them. In reality this may not be the case. By asking questions and having your people articulate the answers, you will be able to determine the extent of their understanding and identify the areas that need to be retaught.

Evaluation should not be a once-in-a-while kind of thing, but a constant, ongoing practice–not if you are going to invest all that you can into other people, and if you expect them to invest themselves in you.

Is This Speaking to You?

Get that certain person's face up close in your mind today. And ask God for the grace to love the way He loves.

PASSING THE TORCH

Responsible leadership requires that you leave your position of power in even better hands than you received it.

THE WORD FOR THE DAY

NO MATTER HOW LONG IT LASTS, OUR TIME OF LEADERSHIP IS SHORT—TOO SHORT TO IGNORE THE NEED FOR TRAINING NEW LEADERS FOR TOMORROW.

CAN YOU NAME ONE EMERGING LEADER YOU WOULD COMMIT TO INVESTING YOURSELF IN?

IN TALKING TO HIS DISCIPLES, JESUS DIDN'T CANDY-COAT THE TASTE OF RESPONSIBILITY. HE PAINTED THE PICTURE IN REAL-LIFE COLORS.

JESUS ALSO ASKED HIS FOLLOWERS TO REPORT BACK TO HIM. BUILD INTO YOUR FOLLOWERS THE ACCOUNTABILITY OF YOUR OWN EVALUATION.

LUKE 10:1-2, 16, 22-24

After this the Lord appointed seventy-two others and sent them two by two ahead of him to every town and place where he was about to go.

He told them, "The harvest is plentiful, but the workers are few. Ask the Lord of the harvest, therefore, to send out workers into his harvest field. . . .

"He who listens to you listens to me; he who rejects you rejects me; but he who rejects me rejects him who sent me. . . .

"All things have been committed to me by my Father. No one knows who the Son is except the Father, and no one knows who the Father is except the Son and those to whom the Son chooses to reveal him."

Then he turned to his disciples and said privately, "Blessed are the eyes that see what you see.

"For I tell you that many prophets and kings wanted to see what you see but did not see it, and to hear what you hear but did not hear it."

LEADERSHIP PRINCIPLE NUMBER 85

QUALITY LEADERS PREPARE FOR THE FUTURE BY TRAINING THEIR SUCCESSORS.

Even though it is almost a cliché in business school to say that a good leader's first duty is to prepare for and train his successor, the reality is that few do. Even knowing that everyone will eventually move on, few leaders follow the example of Jesus and prepare followers for the day they will no longer be on the scene. Too many leaders seem to perpetuate the myth that they are immortal and that their presence is permanent.

Be sure you do not fall into this trap. Sooner or later, you too will move on. Discuss this openly and frankly with your staff. Have a plan in place so that your people are prepared, whether your leaving is unexpected or is more orderly and planned.

Jesus' plan for transition was the most successful in history. He prepared his followers well, openly discussing his eventual departure. They didn't want to see him go, but they were forewarned. They performed spectacularly after Jesus was taken from them, pushing the program to incredible success.

Jesus planned well for his succession. So should you. Your followers and your enterprise deserve it.

Is This Speaking to You?

Stay constantly on the lookout for those in your organization who are showing signs of something greater.

I'M COUNTING ON ME

Some things in your job description don't fall into your list of talents and strengths. But they do fall to you to do them.

THE WORD FOR THE DAY

WHAT DO YOU DO WHEN YOU FEEL OUTMATCHED, OVERSTRESSED, AND UNDERQUALIFIED? THE BEST YOU CAN.

GOD HAS WAYS TO REMIND HIGH ACHIEVERS WHO THE SOURCE OF THEIR STRENGTH IS.

PAUL ACCOMPLISHED A LOT IN HIS MINISTRY—MUCH OF WHICH CAME NATURALLY TO HIS TALENTS AND TEMPERAMENT. BUT HIS GREATEST SUCCESSES WERE THOSE THAT CAME THE HARDEST.

ARE YOU ABLE YET TO "DELIGHT" IN THE PARTS OF YOUR WORK THAT REQUIRE YOU TO STRETCH, TO DIG, TO GROW?

2 CORINTHIANS 11:27-29A, 30, 12:7-10

I have labored and toiled and have often gone without sleep; I have known hunger and thirst and have often gone without food; I have been cold and naked. Besides everything else, I face daily the pressure of my concern for all the churches.

Who is weak, and I do not feel weak? . . . If I must boast, I will boast of the things that show my weakness. . . .

To keep me from becoming conceited because of these surpassingly great revelations, there was given me a thorn in my flesh, a messenger of Satan, to torment me. Three times I pleaded with the Lord to take it away from me.

But he said to me, "My grace is sufficient for you, for my power is made perfect in weakness." Therefore I will boast all the more gladly about my weaknesses, so that Christ's power may rest on me.

That is why, for Christ's sake, I delight in weaknesses, in insults, in hardships, in persecutions, in difficulties. For when I am weak, then I am strong.

LEADERSHIP PRINCIPLE NUMBER 86

LEADERS RECOGNIZE THEIR WEAKNESSES, BUT WORK HARD TO OVERCOME THEM.

Leadership at the highest level almost always demands such a compelling vision that even those closest to us may question our wisdom, even our sanity. If you aspire to leadership, see if you can pass this test: "If my family says I'm nuts, can I still go on?" Jesus did, but certainly not without pain.

There is no tragedy in failing to achieve a certain level of leadership if we face up to the tasks and demands of leadership squarely, honestly, and in an attitude of submission to God's will. If we prayerfully examine opportunities to lead and are then obedient, we will be successful no matter where those opportunities lead us. Tragedies only occur when we fail to take on responsibilities that we are clearly called to fulfill, or when we pursue or demand leadership without objectively and prayerfully examining our ability to lead. When these occur, people are hurt, resources are wasted, and opportunities for growth are impeded.

Are you willing to pay the high price of leadership? Examine yourself. And ask God for the courage to do your best in every situation.

Is This Speaking to You?

The parts of your day which you look forward to the least may be the very ones where you grow the most character.

WHAT ABOUT NOW?

Later is a convenient place to park the tasks of leadership. But there may already be too many cars waiting out there.

THE WORD FOR THE DAY

NOT EVERYTHING THAT CROSSES YOUR DESK IS A PRIORITY ITEM. BUT EVERYTHING MUST BE CHECKED TO SEE IF IT IS.

JAMES CALLED IT "BOASTING" WHEN WE ASSUME THAT TOMORROW WILL BE JUST LIKE TODAY. "WHY, YOU DO NOT EVEN KNOW WHAT WILL HAPPEN TOMORROW." BETTER TO GET AS MUCH DONE TODAY AS WE CAN, AND LEAVE TOMORROW TO THE LORD.

THE WISEST THING TO DO WITH MANY OF THE TASKS YOU FACE MAY INDEED BE TO DELAY THEM. THAT'S NOT PROCRASTINATING. THAT'S BEING PROACTIVE.

JAMES 4:13-17
PROVERBS 3:25-28

Now listen, you who say, "Today or tomorrow we will go to this or that city, spend a year there, carry on business and make money."

Why, you do not even know what will happen tomorrow. What is your life? You are a mist that appears for a little while and then vanishes.

Instead, you ought to say, "If it is the Lord's will, we will live and do this or that."

As it is, you boast and brag. All such boasting is evil. Anyone, then, who knows the good he ought to do and doesn't do it, sins. . . .

Have no fear of sudden disaster or of the ruin that overtakes the wicked, for the LORD will be your confidence and will keep your foot from being snared.

Do not withhold good from those who deserve it, when it is in your power to act. Do not say to your neighbor, "Come back later; I'll give it tomorrow"—when you now have it with you.

LEADERSHIP PRINCIPLE NUMBER 87

PROCRASTINATION WILL CATCH UP WITH YOU WHEN YOU LEAST EXPECT IT.

The strategic decision to delay taking action on a matter is sometimes the wisest move a leader can make. But you and I can easily tell the difference between taking a measured approach and simply putting off an uncomfortable situation.

Procrastination can just about destroy your effectiveness as a leader. The challenges you must deal with on a daily basis are more than enough all by themselves without borrowing from the unaddressed challenges of yesterday and last week. Almost always, the things you avoid out of fear or discomfort will end up causing even more fear and discomfort down the road.

One of the best tactics to use in blunting your tendency to procrastinate is to make a conscious effort to handle your most difficult tasks early in the day–first thing, if possible. If you leave an unpleasant chore off until late in the afternoon, you probably will choose to leave it off till tomorrow. And the domino effect of procrastination rolls on.

Jesus taught us by word and example to deal head-on with problems. We follow Him best when we keep our focus on today.

Is This Speaking to You?

Before you put one more thing off until tomorrow, give the option of doing it today a fair and firm consideration.

HEALTH WISE

The life of a leader calls for eat-out lunches and work-over weekends. That's why it also calls for healthy disciplines.

THE WORD FOR THE DAY

LIFE SETS BEFORE YOU A TRAY OF UNHEALTHY EXPECTATIONS. THAT DOESN'T MEAN YOU HAVE TO BITE.

THE KING'S REGIMEN WENT AGAINST DANIEL'S CONSCIENCE. BUT HE VERY GRACIOUSLY, VERY REASONABLY OBJECTED. YOU DON'T HAVE TO BE PUSHY TO PUSH AWAY FROM THE WORLD'S TABLE.

HEALTHY HABITS CAN CUT INTO YOUR SCHEDULE, BUT ADD YEARS TO YOUR EFFECTIVENESS.

"YOU ARE NOT YOUR OWN; YOU WERE BOUGHT AT A PRICE. THEREFORE HONOR GOD WITH YOUR BODY"

(1 CORINTHIANS 6:19-20)

DANIEL 1:8-10, 12-15

But Daniel resolved not to defile himself with the royal food and wine, and he asked the chief official for permission not to defile himself in this way.

Now God had caused the official to show favor and sympathy to Daniel, but the official told Daniel, "I am afraid of my lord the king, who has assigned your food and drink. Why should he see you looking worse than the other young men of your age? The king would then have my head because of you. . . ."

"Please test your servants for ten days: Give us nothing but vegetables to eat and water to drink. Then compare our appearance with that of the young men who eat the royal food, and treat your servants in accordance with what you see."

So he agreed to this and tested them for ten days.

At the end of the ten days they looked healthier and better nourished than any of the young men who ate the royal food.

LEADERSHIP PRINCIPLE NUMBER 88

COMMIT YOURSELF TO A HEALTHY LIFESTYLE.

Managing our time is perhaps the single greatest challenge we face as busy leaders. One aspect of our lives that suffers most when our schedule continues to conflict is our health.

Much business is conducted over mealtimes, and not always in the most nutritious restaurants in the world. Many of your days as a leader run into long hours that interrupt your exercise regimen. You may feel so worn out by the end of the day that the last thing you want to do when you leave the office is to spend some time on the treadmill or settle for a tossed salad.

But eventually–if not sooner–the neglect we pay to our physical bodies will force them to react in ways that will finally get our attention. It is much easier, even though it doesn't seem so at the time, to take care of our bodies in the midst of our busy schedules than to be controlled by our bodies' limitations after years of unconcern.

I have seen people take physical fitness to an extreme and neglect other important parts of their lives. But God says that our bodies are not our own, and we should care for them as God's property.

Is This Speaking to You?

The Bible says that your body is a temple of the Holy Spirit. You're living in God's house. Don't junk it up.

STEADY, BOYS

You bring so much of yourself into your leadership role. But unchecked emotions can bring your leadership down.

THE WORD FOR THE DAY

1 PETER 4:7-11, 13-14

The end of all things is near. Therefore be clear minded and self-controlled so that you can pray.

Above all, love each other deeply, because love covers over a multitude of sins. Offer hospitality to one another without grumbling.

Each one should use whatever gift he has received to serve others, faithfully administering God's grace in its various forms.

If anyone speaks, he should do it as one speaking the very words of God. If anyone serves, he should do it with the strength God provides, so that in all things God may be praised through Jesus Christ. To him be the glory and the power for ever and ever. Amen. . . .

But rejoice that you participate in the sufferings of Christ, so that you may be overjoyed when his glory is revealed.

If you are insulted because of the name of Christ, you are blessed, for the Spirit of glory and of God rests on you.

TRY TO VIEW YOUR PERSONAL DISPUTES AND DIFFERENCES IN AN ETERNAL LIGHT. WHEN YOU LOSE YOUR TEMPER, IT USUALLY MEANS YOU'VE LOST YOUR PERSPECTIVE.

YOUR LEADERSHIP AND AUTHORITY ARE BUILT ON TRUST. OTHERS MUST BE ABLE TO COUNT ON YOU KEEPING YOUR COOL IN TENSE SITUATIONS.

EMOTIONS ARE NOT BAD. THEIR ENERGY CAN MOTIVATE YOU AND HELP YOU EXCEL.

DON'T TAKE WHAT PEOPLE SAY ABOUT YOU OR YOUR WORK TOO PERSONALLY. LET GOD BE THE JUDGE OF THAT.

LEADERSHIP PRINCIPLE NUMBER 89

LEADERS MUST BE THE MASTERS OF THEIR EMOTIONS.

The Bible offers many examples of men who failed because they lacked the essential element of self-control. The prime example is Samson, the undisputed heavyweight champion of ancient Israel. The key point in the story of Samson was not his problem in the sexual area nearly as much as it was in a lack of emotional control. His most basic problem was that he never learned to control his emotions.

Woody Hayes was one of college football's all-time most successful coaches. His teams at Ohio State University were perennial Big Ten champions and won many Rose Bowl victories. He lost his job and much of the respect he had earned over a long career because he could not control his emotions. He even punched an opposing player during a game.

It is important to know that great inspirational leaders are often emotional people. Emotion is an important motivating force. However, it must be controlled and can never go unchecked. The good news is that through prayer and the power of the Holy Spirit, our emotions can be controlled–no matter how volatile.

Is This Speaking to You?

Get some Bible verses memorized and ready to use against the red flashes of anger and the dead weights of self-doubt.

IN HIS PRESENCE

The safest place in the world to lead is right in the presence of Almighty God. And you are there this very minute.

THE WORD FOR THE DAY

REMEMBER THAT EVEN THE ASPECTS OF YOUR LEADERSHIP WHICH TAKE PLACE BEHIND CLOSED DOORS ARE IN FULL VIEW OF THE EYES OF GOD.

THE BEST WAY TO PREVENT ANGER AND RESENTMENT IS TO FULLY ENTRUST YOUR LEADERSHIP INTO THE HANDS OF GOD. HE WON'T STEER YOU WRONG.

LIVE AND LEAD IN SUCH A WAY THAT GOD'S PRESENCE IS SEEN AS A PRIVILEGE AND PROTECTION INSTEAD OF A PEST.

DO THE BEST YOU CAN. BUT TRUST GOD TO DO WHAT YOU CANNOT.

GENESIS 45:3, 4B-8, 50:20

Joseph said to his brothers, "I am Joseph! Is my father still living?" But his brothers were not able to answer him, because they were terrified at his presence. . . .

"I am your brother Joseph, the one you sold into Egypt!

"And now, do not be distressed and do not be angry with yourselves for selling me here, because it was to save lives that God sent me ahead of you.

"For two years now there has been famine in the land, and for the next five years there will not be plowing and reaping. But God sent me ahead of you to preserve for you a remnant on earth and to save your lives by a great deliverance.

"So then, it was not you who sent me here, but God. He made me father to Pharaoh, lord of his entire household and ruler of all Egypt. . . .

"You intended to harm me, but God intended it for good to accomplish what is now being done, the saving of many lives."

At just the right moment, Joseph's brothers threw him into the cistern. At just the right moment, the Midianites came along. At just the right moment, he was sold to Potiphar. At just the right moment, Potiphar's wife falsely accused him. At just the right moment, he met the baker and the cup bearer. At just the right moment, the cup bearer remembered Joseph. At just the right moment, Pharaoh called for him. At just the right moment, he was promoted to Prime Minister. At just the right moment, Jacob sent his sons to Egypt. At just the right moment, Pharaoh offered them the land of Goshen. At just the right moment, they settled there and prospered.

All of this happened at "just the right moment" and "just the right way" so that the right people would be in the right place so that in the end, everything would come out the way God had ordained in the beginning. God never violated anyone's free will, yet everything happened as He had planned. That is the providence of God in action.

LEADERSHIP PRINCIPLE NUMBER 90

EFFECTIVE LEADERS SEE THE INVISIBLE HAND OF GOD IN EVERY CIRCUMSTANCE OF LIFE.

Is This Speaking to You?

Call out to God for help and direction in your quiet times, but always remember–He is there to help you all the time.

Scripture References Used

OLD TESTAMENT

Genesis 1:31-2:2	*Day 40*
Genesis 6:13-16, 19-22	*Day 79*
Genesis 16:1-6	*Day 56*
Genesis 45:3, 4b-8	*Day 90*
Genesis 50:15-21	*Day 76*
Genesis 50:20	*Day 90*
Exodus 3:10-12a, 13	*Day 38*
Exodus 4:1, 10-13	*Day 38*
Exodus 14:10-14, 21-22	*Day 1*
Exodus 18:14-15, 17-19, 21-22	*Day 54*
Exodus 20:3-4, 7-8, 12-17	*Day 10*
Exodus 20:8-11	*Day 40*
Numbers 14:2-4, 6-9	*Day 22*
Numbers 20:2, 7-12	*Day 77*
Numbers 27:1-8	*Day 72*
Deuteronomy 6:5-9	*Day 47*
Joshua 1:6-11a, 16	*Day 52*
Joshua 9:3-6, 14-16, 19	*Day 6*
Judges 4:15a, 17-21, 23	*Day 3*
Judges 7:2-4a, 5-7	*Day 58*
Judges 7:17-22a	*Day 4*
Ruth 2:17, 19-23a	*Day 19*
1 Samuel 15:12a, 17a, 19, 24-28	*Day 15*
2 Samuel 6:3-9	*Day 67*
2 Samuel 12:1-4, 7, 9, 13	*Day 50*
1 Kings 2:1-4, 10-12	*Day 17*
1 Kings 6:1-2, 11-13, 37-38	*Day 62*
1 Kings 10:1-3, 6-8	*Day 83*
1 Kings 12:1-7	*Day 64*
2 Kings 19:9-10, 14-16, 19	*Day 2*
1 Chronicles 29:1-3, 6	*Day 13*
2 Chronicles 2:3a, 5-9	*Day 11*
Nehemiah 2:4-8	*Day 31*
Nehemiah 4:7-9, 13-15	*Day 42*
Job 2:3-5, 7-10	*Day 8*
Job 42:1-6, 12-13, 16-17	*Day 61*
Psalm 1:1-3	*Day 45*
Psalm 16:1-2, 5-11	*Day 36*
Psalm 19:7-11	*Day 45*
Psalm 37:39-40	*Day 29*
Psalm 66:5, 8-12, 16-20	*Day 39*
Psalm 78:1-8	*Day 27*
Proverbs 3:25-28	*Day 87*
Proverbs 4:13-19, 23-27	*Day 65*
Proverbs 6:20-23	*Day 47*
Isaiah 40:27-31	*Day 29*
Daniel 1:8-10, 12-15	*Day 88*
Jonah 1:1-4, 10, 11b, 15, 17	*Day 33*

NEW TESTAMENT

Matthew 5:38-41, 43-48	*Day 69*
Matthew 6:31-33	*Day 20*
Matthew 10:34-36	*Day 75*
Matthew 20:20-22, 24-28	*Day 44*
Matthew 25:14-21	*Day 71*
Mark 4:35-41	*Day 68*
Mark 6:30-37a	*Day 12*
Mark 12:28-34a	*Day 35*

Scripture References Used

Mark 14:53, 60-62a	*Day 46*
Mark 15:1-5	*Day 46*
Luke 4:23-30	*Day 49*
Luke 9:1-6, 10-11	*Day 34*
Luke 10:1-2, 16, 22-24	*Day 85*
Luke 10:30-34, 36-37	*Day 24*
Luke 10:38-42	*Day 20*
Luke 12:35-38, 42-44	*Day 60*
Luke 14:28-35	*Day 5*
Luke 18:1-8	*Day 14*
John 8:13-14, 25-29	*Day 32*
John 15:9-17	*Day 63*
Acts 8:26-31, 34-35	*Day 25*
Acts 9:19b-22, 26-28	*Day 82*
Acts 15:36-41	*Day 75*
Acts 16:6-10, 13-14	*Day 57*
Romans 12:2-8	*Day 18*
1 Corinthians 2:1-7, 9-10a	*Day 28*
1 Corinthians 5:1-2, 6, 9-12a	*Day 23*
1 Corinthians 12:12	*Day 30*
1 Corinthians 12:31-13:8, 13	*Day 84*
2 Corinthians 3:1-6a,17-18	*Day 9*
2 Corinthians 5:14-20	*Day 26*
2 Corinthians 9:6-8, 10-11, 13a	*Day 66*
2 Corinthians 11:27-29a, 30	*Day 86*
2 Corinthians 12:7-10	*Day 86*
Galatians 2:11-14, 19-20	*Day 53*
Ephesians 4:7, 11-16	*Day 48*
Ephesians 5:1-2, 8-16	*Day 80*
Ephesians 5:25-32	*Day 37*
Philippians 2:19-25, 29-30	*Day 16*
Philippians 4:4-8, 11b-13	*Day 7*
Philippians 4:10, 14-19	*Day 21*
Colossians 1:24-2:1	*Day 41*
Colossians 3:1-4, 12-15	*Day 73*
1 Thessalonians 1:1-3, 2:5-8	*Day 43*
1 Thessalonians 2:5-8	*Day 43*
1 Thessalonians 3:6-12	*Day 74*
2 Thessalonians 3:6-13	*Day 59*
1 Timothy 6:9-10, 17-19	*Day 51*
2 Timothy 1:8-12, 14	*Day 78*
2 Timothy 2:1-6, 15, 22	*Day 70*
2 Timothy 3:1-5, 12-15	*Day 81*
Hebrews 10:19-25	*Day 30*
Hebrews 13:15-21	*Day 55*
James 4:13-17	*Day 87*
1 Peter 4:7-11, 13-14	*Day 89*

NOTES

NOTES

NOTES

NOTES

NOTES

NOTES

NOTES

NOTES